DAVID
BECKHAM

World Cup Heroes.

DAVID BECKHAM

Gwen Russell

JB

JOHN BLAKE

Published by John Blake Publishing Ltd,
3 Bramber Court, 2 Bramber Road,
London W14 9PB, England

www.johnblakepublishing.co.uk

This edition published in paperback in 2010

ISBN: 978 1 84358 173 4

British Library Cataloguing-in-Publication Data:

A catalogue record for this book is available from the British Library.

Design by www.envydesign.co.uk

Printed in Great Britain by CPI Bookmarque, Croydon CR0 4TD

1 3 5 7 9 10 8 6 4 2

Papers used by John Blake Publishing are natural, recyclable products made
from wood grown in sustainable forests. The manufacturing processes
conform to the environmental regulations of the country of origin.

Photos reproduced by kind permission of PA Photos and Rex Features.

1

Ted and Sandra Beckham were ecstatic: they had just had their second child, a son. The year was 1975 and, in early May, Sandra entered Whipps Cross Hospital in Leytonstone, east London where, on the second day of that month, she gave birth to David Robert Joseph Beckham, who was to be the second of three children – Lynne, the oldest, was born a couple of years earlier and Joanna was yet to come along. And Ted, in particular, was delighted, for the arrival of a boy meant he had someone with whom to share his deepest and most abiding interest – football.

All his life, Ted had worshipped Manchester United, and from the start he was determined his newborn would share his passion. At first, of course, no one had any idea quite how much his son was to fulfil his dreams, for the Beckhams came from humble origins: Sandra was a hairdresser and Ted a kitchen fitter, with no idea that their son was one day going to become one of the most famous men in the world. But what they would soon know was that baby Becks would become just as fanatical about the sport as his father was.

From a very young age, David was taken by Ted to a nearby park for a kickabout and the boy soon became so keen on this new pastime that he would practise alone for hours and hours, perfecting the dead-ball kicks that are now world famous. As an adult, David once revealed that some people thought his famous free kicks were a matter of luck: they were not, he said. They were the result of unending practice stints that dated back to those very early days.

Shortly after David's birth, the family moved to Chingford, Essex, the home of his grandparents, where he was to spend the remainder of his childhood. Always an appealing little boy, David seemed to have only one drawback as far as football was concerned – his height. It was not until his late teens that he suddenly shot up to become the six-footer that he is now.

If David worried about his height, he didn't show it. Football became such a passion, so quickly, that it soon dominated his entire life. He would play wherever he could: not only in spaces just outside his family's houses, but also on the council pitches at Ainsley Wood School.

Away from the pitch, he was surprisingly shy. It's a quality he's retained to this day: when he first met the then Victoria Adams, it was she who had to open the conversation.

David's first school was Chase Lane Primary School and fellow schoolmates remember his passion for football even back then. 'We were all very quiet at school, David especially,' recalls Matthew Treglohan, who became one of David's closest friends. 'I used to sit next to him in geography and art classes. He was very good at art, but was only ever interested in football. He wasn't even that bothered about girls then. A few of the kids shone through in football, but David was certainly one of the best.'

It was while he was attending Chingford School that David took the first step towards what was to become his career. The local paper ran an ad reading: 'Wanted: Football stars of the future'. (Ironically, in one of the many parallels that run throughout their lives, Victoria also kicked off her career when she spotted an ad for singers and dancers in a paper, although in her case she was in her late teens.) David got in touch and soon began playing for the Ridgeway Rovers in the Enfield Sunday League. The team, David's local outfit, played in what is now called the Peter May Sports Ground in Wadham Road, Highams Park. It is fair to say he made his mark: in the course of three years, he scored over 100 goals, while also playing for another team, Chingford High, in the Waltham Forest District and Essex Under-15s.

A fellow school footballer, Nana Boachie, remembers it well. 'We were both 11 in our first proper football contest and David desperately wanted to start off with a goal,' Nana says. 'As goalie on the opposing side, I wanted to keep a clean sheet. He just said, "We'll see," in that quiet voice of his. Just before half-time, we gave away a free kick just outside the area. David curled the ball into the top corner. It was impossible to save. He still remembers it.'

So proficient did the young David show himself to be that top clubs began to notice him. He might have been only 11, but London clubs Tottenham Hotspur and Arsenal both began making enquiries about this extraordinarily talented young man. But, despite the fact that he lived just outside London, David wasn't interested.

He knew who he wanted to play for and it wasn't a London club at all – it was Manchester United. Ted Beckham was a stalwart fan of United and now his son was, too.

'I used to take so much stick from my mates at school,' David confessed. 'I had a couple of mates who were West Ham fans and a couple who were Tottenham or Arsenal fans. But I remember when we beat Arsenal 6–2, Sharpey [Lee Sharpe] scored the hat-trick. I used to wear my United shirt over my school uniform on my way to school, so I got a lot of stick, but I used to give a lot back.'

It is noticeable, incidentally, that even then David was going to wear what he wanted, regardless of what anyone else thought. Indeed, he was to become interested in clothes very early on. But, to fund that habit and much else besides, he had to earn some money and so got a job as a potman at Walthamstow Dog Stadium, where he earned the princely sum of £10 a night. And it was at this young age that David got a taste of what was to come. In 1986, he took part in the TSB Bobby Charlton Soccer Skills final, which he won – the youngest competitor ever to have done so. And that final took place at Old Trafford, Manchester United's home ground, which meant that David first kicked a ball there when he was only 11. Funnily enough, the prize was also a little taste of what was to come: a two week trip to Spain to train with Barcelona. Terry Venables was the manager and players included Mark Hughes, Steve Archibald and Gary Lineker.

Nor was that the only foretaste of what his later life was to be like. The competition at Old Trafford took place on the same day as a match with Tottenham Hotspur, and so there were plenty of Spurs fans present. Despite David's tender years, the fans were not shy about making clear what they thought of his choice of team. 'All the Spurs fans were there and, as I was doing the dribbling in and out of the cones, they noticed that this was David Beckham of Essex,' he said. 'The Spurs fans started singing and cheering, but then the announcer said I was a Man United fan. They booed me and I went in to a couple of cones.'

It was fortunate that David was showing such promise on the pitch, because he certainly wasn't shining at school. Blessed with only limited academic ability, he clearly spent most of his time in lessons wishing he could get out of them, as evidenced by a number of tersely worded school reports dating from when he was 12. 'David is continually silly, which he cannot afford to be if he wishes to make progress,' his French teacher wrote. 'I can only hope for a more mature approach.'

The French teacher was not alone: none of the others seemed to rate David's abilities very highly either. 'His behaviour has been extremely silly,' thundered the doyenne of Home Economics. 'Could do a lot better.'

'David has ability but finds it difficult to concentrate,' wrote his Humanities teacher. 'His attitude must improve immediately if he is to fulfil his potential.'

Indeed, it would appear that the only field he was excelling in was the playing field – but even here he came in for criticism. 'David has a natural ability to succeed at most sports,' said his sports teacher, in a reflection that was to prove emphatically correct. 'But he should be careful of distractions, which affect his application.'

As for David himself? 'I would have enjoyed lessons at

school more if we'd talked about football,' he said. 'But I was quite good at art – maybe I'd have gone into that if I had not got my break in soccer.'

If truth be told, David was never destined for academia. His greatest enjoyment when confined to the classroom was causing disruption, not swotting for his exams, and his friends felt the same way too. 'To be honest, teachers used to find David and his friends hard to control,' said a teacher who had once taught at the school. 'He and six or seven of his cronies were together in the same class. They caused quite a few problems. The girls were very bright, very hardworking. But the boys wouldn't listen or pay attention. There'd be paper flicking or jostling around. David would be in the middle of that somewhere. They were boys straight out of a comic at times.'

Outside of school, however, the older generation was taking a very different attitude to the young Beckham. Winning the competition at Old Trafford and his subsequent spell in Barcelona had made him keener than ever on all things football, and the clubs continued to circle. Tottenham Hotspur was still keen and enticed David to spend some time with its school of excellence. Leyton Orient also offered him a trial. And, finally, the great Manchester United joined in: their talent scout, Malcolm Fidgeon, had heard talk of a remarkably talented young footballer resident in Essex and so attended a match in which David was playing for the Waltham Forest Under-12s against Redbridge. David's mother found out about Fidgeon's presence and alerted her son that a very big opportunity indeed might have presented itself.

'I leaped into the air and started to cry,' said David. 'It

was a dream come true. It was one of my best games for the district. Being from London and being a southerner, I never thought I would get seen by a scout of Man United. But then I was lucky enough one day and I had a good game for my district side. I remember getting changed and I walked out and my mum called me over – my dad was working. There was excitement in her voice when she said, "It's lucky you had a good game, because there was a scout here from Man United and he wants to talk to Dad to discuss taking you to the club for trials."'

It was a dream come true, not only for David, but for his father too. The fact that there was a chance that his son was to play with the team he supported was as exciting an event as anything that had happened in his life up until now. David was pretty excited too and, when he was just 14, he signed up as a schoolboy associate of United. The club itself, of course, did not yet realise quite what a treasure they had in their hands, but hopes were high right from the start.

'David is a good prospect,' said a United spokesman. 'We are delighted that he is joining us.'

It was one of those rare moments in life where just about everyone involved had got what they wanted.

Until then, David's most important footballing mentor had been his father, but now he was to meet the man who transformed him from amateur to professional. Eric Harrison was the youth coach at United and as such was to take charge of the young Beckham's progress. Indeed, Harrison's input to David's career should not be underestimated: it was he, quite as much as Sir Alex Ferguson, who turned David into the player he is today.

Harrison was modest about his abilities. 'A good football coach is like a good school teacher – they realise the youngsters are the important ones,' he said. 'We do it for the kids, not for our own egos. I have taken so much pleasure from seeing young players develop both as footballers and people. David Beckham might have funny haircuts and lead a different life from the rest of us, but the important thing is he's a really good kid as well. Respect was a word I used all the time to Beckham, Giggs and the other players at United. We as adult coaches respect the youngsters and in return the youngsters should also be respectful. I am a hard taskmaster and never let the kids at United step out of line or become arrogant. Players should be confident, yes, but not arrogant where they think they know it all.'

David took these lessons and a good deal more to heart. Something else that he has in common with Victoria is that both were absolutely focused on what they wanted to do in their careers from a very early age and, to this end, David was different from his peer group. While they went out and partied, he stayed home and trained. 'I gave up a lot when I was younger, going out with the lads, parties and discos, leaving my family,' he said. 'It wasn't easy, but I knew it was what I wanted to do. I used to tell everyone and they'd laugh and say, "Yeah, but what else you gonna do?" I'd say, "No, football." United was the dream.'

Football was not the only sport in which David was competing and winning. Four years in a row he won the Essex 1500 metre championship, impressing everyone with his stamina and determination. Other clubs continued to try to tempt him away from his beloved United, but he wasn't having any of it. Wimbledon was one: manager Joe Kinnear tried hard to get him to Selhurst Park, Wimbledon's home ground at the time, but with no luck. 'Beckham must have been about 15,' said Kinnear. 'He was a quiet lad but obviously mad on football and I wanted him. But he told me he had his heart set on going to Old Trafford.'

Indeed, he had and he finally did so in 1991, at the age of 16. It was a tender age to be leaving home, especially for a shy young man like David, but he was to realise a lifelong dream: the beginning of his career at Old Trafford. Not that anyone realised quite how auspicious a career it was going to be, though there were hints, according to Annie Kay who, with her husband Tommie, gave David digs when he first went to Manchester. Firm United supporters and now in their seventies, the Kays had been providing lodgings for young Manchester United players for 30 years.

'When David first came down, I never thought this could be the future England captain,' Annie Kay recalled. 'Having said that, he was always dedicated and a very smart dresser. When he came with his clothes, he had brought seven bags – most young footballers just had two. I said, "You've got some bags!" He said, "I've got some more!" He was very clothes conscious even when he was 16 and stood out in the neighbourhood. The girls loved him, but he wasn't bothered. He'd always be very friendly and always talk but he was very keen on his football. There was not much time for girlfriends.'

It is usually Victoria who is credited for turning David into the male fashion icon he is today but, according to Annie, David may well have managed it without her. 'Victoria has improved him a bit, but he was very fashion-conscious before he ever met her,' Annie recalls. 'He was never a slob. He was always picky and he'd sort his own room out. He said, "Give me my bedding and I'll change my bed." There wasn't a thing out of place in his room. Not like some of the others we've had here. I'd give Mark Hughes his shirts and everything and he'd drop them on the floor. I'd pick him up but he'd say, "I know where everything is if it's on the floor."'

The Kays' house was right next to The Cliff in Salford, where United used to train at the time. And the digs were a find. David had actually stayed in two other places before coming upon the Kays, both of which he'd had to leave – the first because one of his fellow players behaved badly and David got caught up in the row, and the second because he didn't like the food, which didn't go down well with his landlady. But, with the Kays, he found a real home from home, one which was to nurture him while his real family was back in the south.

David is well aware of how lucky he was. 'My third home in Manchester is the one that holds the greatest affection,' he wrote in *David Beckham: My World*, the first of his autobiographies. 'It was the home in Lower Broughton of the terrific Annie and Tommie Kay. Mark Hughes, a legend in my eyes, stayed in the room that I had for a number of years.'

Indeed, the Mark Hughes connection was what had initially attracted him to the Kays. 'This was the one place he wanted to come to because Mark Hughes was here and he was his hero,' Annie recalled. 'What a prospect! I didn't know he had the talent then, but he was something special. He lived and breathed football and never got injured.'

It was also the perfect place for a young footballer to grow up. 'It was just like being an addition to their own family – and the great thing, especially for a teenager, was that they allowed me to have my own space,' David wrote.

Not that David was exactly a tearaway. He hadn't got this far to throw away the stunning opportunities now afforded to him and was training just as hard as ever without going wild on the side. Indeed, the only indulgences he allowed himself were, inevitably, fashion and shopping out of his £29.50 weekly wage – something his team-mates were quick to pick up.

'He's always been a flash Cockney,' said Ryan Giggs, one of David's fellow players. 'Even at 17 when we all had Honda Preludes, he had a leather interior and a personalised licence plate.'

Another team-mate was Gary Neville. 'I still remember coming across him in the youth teams,' he recalled. 'All of us local lads, such as Nicky Butt, me and Paul Scholes, wondered who this flash Cockney was. He always used to have the latest United tracksuit and the club clearly rated him.'

Nor was David the only exceptional talent coming on board. David and his team-mates came variously to be known as Fergie's Fledglings or The Class of '92, simply because of the mass of new talent now at the club: others included the Neville brothers, Nicky Butt, Ryan Giggs (who featured in a poster Victoria stuck up on her wall in the very earliest days of the Spice Girls) and Paul Scholes.

Whatever might have happened since, it was a coup on the part of Alex Ferguson. Indeed, he allowed himself to be quietly pleased about the quality of the players he had brought on board, and, in an interview shortly after Keith Gillespie hit the headlines after a stunning match against Bury, and a few months after United won the FA Youth Cup, he said as much.

'There are more like Keith in our youth team and we are looking closely at them,' he confided. 'We don't like to go overboard about young players, but this lot are very exciting. With their ability and desire to play, they should go far. Winning the FA Youth Cup can be significant. When United last won it in 1964, it triggered the best period in the club's post–Munich period. We have 18 trainees and every one of them will be given a full professional contract at 18. We don't have any doubt about them making their mark in the game. To have them all come through like this is very rare. Now it's just a matter of fitting them into the first team when the occasion arises.'

Even so, although David was clearly a very gifted player, it took some time before he was allowed to prove himself on the pitch. During his first year, when he wasn't training, he and his fellow trainees were expected to do menial tasks such as cleaning the older footballers' boots. And it took a whole year before he was finally allowed out on the field: in 1992 he was brought on as a substitute for Andrei Kanchelskis in the League Cup tie against Brighton. The game ended 1–1 and four months later David made another step closer to his ultimate dream when he signed his professional contract.

Alex Ferguson wasn't the only one to be aware of the quality of his players. Bobby Charlton, who had been the David Beckham of his day and who was now a director of United, was equally impressed by all the talent now in the team. 'People say Alex should be handed the Old Trafford manager's job for life if he brings us the title this season for the first time in 26 years,' he said. 'But he already has the job for as long as he wants it. He deserves it for all the work he has put in at Old Trafford in the last six years and not just with the first team.

'What really impresses me about Manchester United under Alex's management is not the way the first team are playing – it's the future that fills me with such confidence. Of course, we fancy our chances of taking the title this season. It's going to be either us, Aston Villa or Blackburn. But I fancy our chances just as strongly in the FA Youth Cup, which we won last season. We are already in the fourth round against Wimbledon and I'm certain we'll go all the way again. That's how highly I rate the kids Alex has brought into the club.

'I've never known us – or any club in England – to have so many potentially brilliant youngsters. We have so many we are actually having to turn some very talented teenagers away. When I see these kids, I get really excited. They are an absolute joy, the way they play. Five or six of this year's youth team are certain to fix in the Premier League in the next couple of seasons. They are already that good.'

With such an array of dazzling talent to compete with, perhaps it's not surprising that David was still not outshining the rest. If anything, he wasn't coming along as fast as some of his peers, which was one reason that Ferguson decided to loan him out to Preston for a month in early 1995. It was to prove to be the making of him, although David certainly didn't think so at the time.

'I definitely didn't want to go – that's nothing against

Preston,' he said. 'I was gutted really because I felt my career was over at Manchester United. The manager assured me it wasn't and it's the best thing I've ever done in my career, going to Preston. I scored straight from a corner on my debut and from a free kick in my second game, so things went quite well.'

What David really needed was to be toughened up, and the spell at Preston did exactly that. Gary Neville, who was fast becoming David's best friend, said as much. 'We all knew he had great ability but people said he was a bit soft going into tackles and headers. Going into the Third Division with Preston and having people kick lumps out of him toughened him up.'

And not only did it toughen him up, it showed him that there were distinct advantages in playing for Manchester United. 'Usually you walk into United and your kit's laid out, nice brand-new towel, nice clean everything – underwear, shorts, the lot,' he later recalled. 'I turned up there and there was nothing. They had to give me odds and sods from all over the place.' And worse was to come – he had to wash his own kit.

And it was while he was with Preston that the David Beckham of today first really began to emerge. Although he was only there for a month, he scored twice, and one of those goals was the first time anyone had seen one of his trademark free kicks.

After that, Ferguson felt David and the rest of the youngsters were finally ready to make their mark, and so set about getting them on to the team. To make room, Andrei Kanchelskis, Paul Ince and Mark Hughes were sold.

David was utterly overwhelmed. 'When I was coming

through the ranks, I didn't see any light at the end of the tunnel for me because there was Andrei who was flying,' he said. 'Then, all of a sudden, the door opened when the manager sold them and got us youngsters in.'

History was to prove that Sir Alex had made exactly the right move, but at the time many commentators were appalled. Among them was Alan Hansen, himself a former footballer and now a commentator on BBC's *Match of the Day*, who made his disquiet known, saying, 'You can't win anything with kids.'

Sir Alex – and Bobby Charlton – knew otherwise.

It was the start of an exhilarating time for Beckham. In April 1995, he left Preston to return to the team and soon after made his Premier League debut in a match against Leeds United. His form improved steadily and then, to the great joy of everyone involved, he managed to score the winning goal against Chelsea in the FA Cup semi-final. Ted was as jubilant as his son: it was a dream come true for both of them.

And the fact that there was so much talent out there on the Manchester United pitch merely served to push the players further. Each wanted to be the best and the fact that the competition was so intense made them compete even harder. David trained hard, played hard and kept to the straight and narrow and, in August 1996, he was finally rewarded with the goal that made his name. Ironically, it was at Selhurst Park against Wimbledon, the very club that had tried to get David on board some years earlier when he was still barely more than a child. The goal in question was a beauty scored from the halfway line to beat Neil Sullivan, who was out in front of his area.

'It changed my life,' said David. 'The ball seemed to be in the air for hours and it all went quiet. Then the ball went in and it just erupted. I was on cloud nine. I just wanted to shake everyone's hand and stay out on the pitch for half an hour.'

That goal did quite a number of things. It strengthened the bond between Sir Alex and his young protégé – for it was at around this time that Ferguson almost seemed to be a second father to David. He was proud of the young Beckham for his dedication and talent, and anxious to encourage him to ascend the very heights of the game. It also attracted the attention of another man, one who was to play an extremely influential role in David's future career. That man was the then England manager Glenn Hoddle, who was incredibly impressed by what he saw out there on the field that day. A month later, David made his England debut against Moldova.

It is difficult to overstate quite how well David was doing at this juncture. By the end of the 1996/7 season, he had played in all the World Cup qualifying games; he had been voted the PFA Young Player of the Year; he had reached the European Cup semi-finals; and his beloved Manchester United had won both the Premiership and the FA Cup in 1996. He was quite clearly a major star in the making.

But, for all that, David was still well known only among the footballing community. He had a certain flashiness about him, certainly, but there was no indication of what was to come. There was no jewellery back in those days, apart from the odd glitzy watch, and there was certainly no nail polish or talk of facials. David was still a straightforward young man with a brilliant career to look

forward to, and on top of that there was no conflict at all between him and Sir Alex Ferguson. They both wanted David to be the best and he was doing everything in his power to get there. But the time was fast approaching when there was going to be a change in all of this. David was not far off from the most significant meeting of his life. Indeed, in the theatre that was now his life, it would be fair to say there was a pop star waiting in the wings.

2

David might have been succeeding beyond all expectation at his chosen career, but to his very great credit he was managing to retain a sense of proportion. David has always had an innate modesty and this was clearly manifesting itself as he began to adjust to the knowledge that he was becoming a star.

'You cannot afford to let things go to your head,' he said. 'First of all you'd get hammered by the other lads, then you have to face up to the boss. The first sign that you're getting carried away and he comes down on you like a ton of bricks. I know how difficult it's been just breaking into the first team and I'm not going to do anything to put that at risk. On the pitch sometimes it's beyond your control but it's down to you and I would be stupid to think I'm something special.'

Sir Alex was clearly a key figure in keeping the boys' feet on the ground, but David was also aware that he was following in the footsteps of some very illustrious predecessors.

'Anyway, how can someone as inexperienced as me try

to be big-time when I look at the players alongside me?' he continued. 'They've probably forgotten more than I'll ever know. People like Peter Schmeichel, Eric Cantona and Gary Pallister have won just about everything going – and all I've done is scratch the surface. Hopefully, in a few years I will be able to sit back and think I've achieved something, but at the moment I'm just struggling to hold down a first-team place.'

But it was becoming quite clear that David was turning into a world-class player and others in the field had no doubts about what a coming star they had on their hands.

'Different class,' said Graham Rix, who was working with Glenn Hoddle to train the young England players. 'You can look at players of that age and tell the ones who will fail and who will make it, and those who will be stars. Becks is going to be a true star. Everybody knows what he can do with a ball at his feet, but that's not as important as what goes on away from game situations. Tell him something in training and it's done instantly; ask him to do something and there's no moans, raised eyebrows or questions, he just does it.

At this stage in his career, David was still very much deferring to the older and more established players. He didn't yet have the confidence he gained when he linked up with Victoria and gave the impression of being very much in awe of the company in which he found himself. He practically hero-worshipped Eric Cantona.

'You can't put into words what Eric means to us,' he said. 'Just having him on the pitch wearing a red shirt is more of a boost than you could ever explain. Other teams are frightened of him, I'm convinced of that. They know

how dangerous he can be and that is worth a goal start to us. He's also been brilliant with the young players. He doesn't say too much, stand up at the blackboard and give us coaching lessons or anything, but a simple word of advice now and again often means more than a thousand coaching sessions. You only play with people like that once in your career. My hero was Bryan Robson. I wasn't around when he was at his best, but I'm just as proud to say I played in the same team as Eric Cantona.'

Of course, David did have a life outside of football, although until then it had very much taken second place to his career. One early girlfriend was Leoni Marzell, who, like David, came from Essex and she made a very telling comment about where her boyfriend's interests lay. 'He'd rather talk about Arsenal all night with my dad than enjoy a bedroom romp with me,' she remarked.

David also had relationships with Anna Bartley and Julie Killilea, but neither was particularly serious – he was merely a young man having fun. But the position of women in his life was about to make a radical change in 1997, when he first met the artist then known as Posh Spice.

It is now often forgotten that, when David and Victoria first met, she was the massively famous superstar and he was the young ingénue. The Spice Girls, one of the most successful girl groups ever, had launched themselves the previous year and, while no one seemed to be quite sure who they were or where they had come from, everyone seemed keen to buy their records. Behind the scenes and away from the chat about Girl Power and snogging boys, the show was being run with military efficiency by the girls' manager, Simon Fuller, and their record label, Virgin, but, fronting the show, the girls were having a whale of a time. And when a Spice Girl met a footballer, theirs seemed to be the perfect match in a celebrity-obsessed age.

The actual meeting first took place in March 1997. Victoria wasn't interested in football, but her fellow Spice Girl Mel C was and she decided to attend a match at Old Trafford with Simon Fuller. Knowing David would be playing, Victoria decided to accompany them. David's first clue that there was someone he might want to meet in the crowd came when said crowd started booing – because Mel C supported Liverpool. After asking what was going on, David, to his utter delight, was informed that two of the Spice Girls were present.

'I jumped up and said, "Which ones? Which ones?" But whoever said it couldn't remember. And it was a struggle to get my mind back on the match.'

Even though he was desperate to meet her, David very nearly blew his chances in the players' bar afterwards. Victoria and Mel were holding court: paralysed with shyness, David didn't have the courage to approach the object of his desire. It was left to Victoria to make the first move, which she did with aplomb, strolling up to him and asking, 'Good game?'

And so showbusiness history was made.

At first the relationship was kept secret, because everyone involved realised that the story, when it broke, would be enormous. That, incidentally, was entirely because of Victoria's celebrity. Back then, when David was just another up-and-coming footballer, Posh's privacy had to be protected and, so, for their first date, the two ended up in Mel C's flat.

'For the first three dates he was so shy he didn't kiss me,' said Victoria. 'He finally got round to it while we were at my parents' house after our fourth date. It was worth the wait.'

Back in 1997, news of the relationship slowly began to seep out, as it was inevitable that it would. They were seen in a nightclub together, after which it became known that Victoria had introduced David to her parents. 'Everything in her life is wonderful at the moment,' said mum Jackie Adams. 'She's on top of the world. We've been told not to talk about David.'

Like Victoria, David felt that their joint celebrity was a help rather than a hindrance to the relationship.

'That's normal,' he said of the publicity the two were attracting. 'I'm a footballer and she's a Spice Girl. It would be silly if we did not think the media and public were attracted to us. But we are just two normal young people going out together. It helps that Victoria is famous. It helps with the pressure if she is involved, because we both share it. We do understand the pressure, even though we are only 22 and 23. We are learning together. I don't see myself as front-page news but going out with Victoria I am going to get it. It is something we must handle.'

And handle it they did – rather well, in fact. As David's profile soared, the lucrative sponsorship deals that have contributed so strongly to the couple's wealth began to pour in. The first was a deal with Brylcreem, for which David was paid £1 million. He was earning rather more on the pitch than he had been as a trainee too, given that he was now being paid £10,000 a week. There were clear signs that he was beginning to enjoy the finer things in life: a Cartier was the start of a serious watch collection, while high street labels were being replaced by the designer variety.

David was a tiny bit concerned at the effect all of this might have on his image but, if truth be told, he could handle that too. 'I know that dating Victoria has doubled the interest in me. We like to go for quiet meals together, but we always seem to be photographed shopping. I sometimes think people must think I live in Gucci and Prada shops. I worry that fans will forget I play football as well as go out with a Spice Girl. But I've turned down a lot of sponsorship offers because I want to be known as a footballer.'

One person who had most certainly not forgotten that David was a footballer and who was far from pleased about recent developments was Sir Alex Ferguson. His relationship with David up until now really had been as a surrogate father, but, as the fuss surrounding Posh and Becks intensified, Sir Alex became increasingly concerned about the effect it would have on David's football. In a very short space of time, David had gone from being a footballer known mainly in sporting circles to one half of the most high-profile couple in the world and Ferguson didn't like it one bit. He wanted his boys to train hard, take proper rest and have a bit of fun at the weekends. What was happening to David was something else all together. And so, like the bad fairy at the feast, he made his displeasure known – in this case, of course, on the football pitch.

The very first indication that all was not well between Beckham and his mentor came in August 1997, just five months after David and Victoria first met. Sir Alex had become increasingly irritable about the amount of time

David spent on his mobile to his new girlfriend, but until now that irritation was kept on the training pitch. Now it spilled out in public when Ferguson dropped David from a match against Chelsea at Wembley and sent him to play in a friendly against Bournemouth instead.

The rest of the world had hitherto been unaware of the problems fermenting in the dressing room, and reacted with a mixture of shock and dismay.

'David is a world-class player and this is an insult to him,' said Tommy Docherty, who had himself been a manager at Manchester United. 'I think the young man has handled himself superbly. Ferguson says that you take a long term view on players. It's lucky that Brazil didn't take a long term view on Pele. Beckham has been an absolute model pro. He's a good lad and this decision doesn't make sense.'

But it did in Ferguson's eyes. In his view, David was putting his girlfriend before his football and so he should be punished on the football pitch. Not that he put it like that publicly, of course. He merely commented, 'I was concerned about the tournament at the end of the last season in France. There is a price to pay for it. Gary Neville admitted to me that he felt really tired before he even went there.

'As far as David is concerned, we are fortunate in having a tremendous midfield of Paul Scholes, Nicky Butt and Roy Keane. I can add David when I feel the time is right, in two or three weeks. I believe we're doing the right thing for him. He is still immature as a player. He has still got a frame to fill – he will add a few more pounds. He is a later developer than some of the other young players. We will keep an eye on him.'

And so there was yet another constant in the

relationship between David and Victoria – the disapproval of Sir Alex Ferguson was in there right from the start.

Though David and Victoria as a whole were becoming an even greater attraction than the sum of their parts, David remained as conscientious a player as he had always been and he was becoming more successful than ever on the pitch. 'That [the 1996/7 season] was the best of my career, so I've sat down with my dad and the manager to talk about how to keep it at that level,' David said. 'We all feel I can still get better. Alex Ferguson told me to rest a lot, practise a lot, look after myself and, most importantly, just concentrate on my football and nothing else.'

As the relationship grew stronger still, David was increasingly candid about how he and Victoria managed to cope. 'We take every opportunity to enjoy our privacy. We'd like a little more. But we know we are high-profile people. It would be the same for me whatever I did because of Victoria's business. We would like to lead normal lives and do things that don't get noticed. But I have put myself in that situation because of what I am doing on the field. Now it is a case of dealing with what happens off it.'

Soon the news leaked out that the two were talking about getting engaged. In Germany for the premiere of *SpiceWorld: The Movie*, Victoria said, 'We are soon getting married. As soon as Gucci makes clothes for expectant mums, I would even consider a pregnancy.'

In lieu, perhaps, of actual babies, the couple bought a pair of Rottweiler puppies, which rejoiced in the names Puff Daddy and Snoop Doggy Dogg. Christmas rolled round and with it the lavish gift giving for which the two came to be known: David gave Victoria a £13,000 jewel-studded cross and received in return an £11,000 gold and diamond bracelet.

The actual Christmas celebrations took place in a Manchester hotel and it is notable that Victoria's parents attended and David's didn't. But the two young superstars were in no mood to worry about that, for they had decided that, despite the fact that they had known one another for less than a year, they would definitely be getting married. David booked a room at the Rookery Hall Hotel in Nantwich, Cheshire, for the night of 24 January 1998, and it was here that he finally asked Victoria to be his bride. When Victoria arrived, she was presented with 30 roses and then escorted up to the room, which David had filled with red and yellow roses and lilies costing £200. The setting and the scene could not have been more romantic.

The news was made public the next day – indeed, the two staged an impromptu press conference outside the hotel – and, while no one who knew them well was surprised, just about everyone was delighted (although David's father, tellingly, had not yet heard the news when the press told him about it and he refused to comment).

David himself couldn't wait. 'Gary Neville will be my best man,' he said. 'He's my best mate and was the man who first knew how I felt about Victoria. He'll already be getting nervous about his speech. The boss will be pleased. He doesn't interfere in our private lives. He just wants me to make sure I keep myself fit and he trusts me.'

David was being wildly optimistic. Sir Alex did indeed like his boys to settle down young, believing it grounded them, but his ideal of a wife for a Manchester United player was emphatically not Victoria Adams.

3

The news of Victoria and David's engagement made headlines around the world. The Spice Girls were still enormously successful, while David's star was also on the rise. His involvement with Victoria had raised his profile enormously, while at the same time his skill on the pitch seemed to be increasing almost by the hour. Just a couple of days after announcing his engagement, United beat Chelsea 5–3, with David scoring two of the goals. It seemed the golden boy of soccer could do no wrong.

That January there was also a foretaste of what else was to come. David accompanied Victoria to the Versace fashion show in Milan, a clear indication of where his interests lay off the field.

Now a seriously hot property, David continued to attract those increasingly lucrative sponsorship deals. The latest was with Adidas, in an unprecedented seven-year £4 million arrangement. On top of that, he was earning £20,000 a week and was now worth an estimated £10 million. But this did not meet with joy from all quarters and inevitably there were some fears that all this might start going to David's head.

He insisted that would not be the case. 'A lot has been made about me supposedly getting too big for my boots,' he said. 'But the people who know me know that isn't true. A lot of things have changed in my life – but the way I am hasn't. I have a lot of people who will knock me down if I do change. Alex Ferguson hasn't said, "Cut it out," because he doesn't think I'm doing anything wrong. He has told me I'm handling everything well. Glenn Hoddle doesn't see a problem either. And the other players don't.'

But, as his fame increased, so did the aggravation that went with it. His car was stolen and then burned. Someone began stalking him and then, worse still, someone sent bullets through the post with David's name on them. It was a deeply upsetting experience and was the first of many occasions when he had to increase the security surrounding him and his family, and it may well also have been the reason that he started showing an on-field characteristic that was nearly to ruin him – a bad temper.

The first sign that David's temper might be about to cause problems came in a match against Chelsea. There was a flare-up on the pitch and David was given a yellow card. Glenn Hoddle, who was at that time England manager, was not pleased: the World Cup was only a few months away and he wanted to ensure all his team were absolutely ready for the tournament. Flare-ups on the pitch were not what he wanted at all. 'David got booked again needlessly and we have to talk,' he snapped. 'He had a similar problem for us in Le Tournoi last year and we can't afford that sort of behaviour at the World Cup finals this summer.'

David, as the world now knows, did not heed that very good advice.

However, off the pitch he seemed as grounded as ever. He might have been a megastar, but he certainly wasn't about to go all grand on the back of it. 'The other day I was round at Victoria's house and the postman rang the bell to deliver something,' he said. 'I went and answered the door and his jaw dropped. "Blimey," he said, "I never thought I'd see a legend this early in the morning." But that's just daft. I'm only 22. I haven't done anything.'

David could not quite believe just how excited everyone got about his appearance, his life and, indeed, just him. 'It's a shame that my new hairstyle can make the front of the papers when there's so many more important things going on in the world,' he said. 'It shocks me. There's kids all over the world that are losing lives and losing families and then because I've gone blond it's on the front of the paper. It's not my fault.'

But, despite this modest attitude, flare-ups did continue on the pitch. Perhaps, in retrospect, they were the making of him. The stress had been getting to him, not only in terms of dealing with his fame, but also when it came to the pressure to succeed.

'The first time I really got into the squad, the manager wasn't using me a lot,' he recalled. 'I was on the bench and sometimes I wasn't even getting changed. That kept me hungry. I always wanted to be there. And, once I got a taste for it, I felt sort of embarrassed if I wasn't there. When I got to Manchester, I didn't want people down in London saying, "Oh, he'll be back in a couple of years because he's crap. And I was worried they would also be saying that I hadn't made the standard. It was a sort of embarrassment.'

But it was also an impetus to push himself hard – and David did.

There were, of course, massive compensations as well, and one of them was the money. David and Victoria now made their first really significant property purchase: a £300,000 penthouse flat in Alderley Edge, Cheshire.

David also chose this moment to bring out the first of his autobiographies, entitled *My Story*. He was pretty young to be writing his life story, and this was perhaps why the book was as notable for all the pictures of him it contained as for any life experience. After all, he was still a year away from getting married.

As rival fans began to absorb the figure he'd become, so they turned their attentions towards David's private life and, in particular, his bride-to-be. They had taken to singing songs about what the couple got up to after lights out, and they weren't being that complimentary. 'It's pretty difficult when you're young and you're getting that sort of stick off crowds,' said David with commendable understatement. 'It's hard to get used to. It's not as if they're saying it about your football, they're saying it about your private life. But every time they've said it, I've gone and scored.'

Then there was that other crucial relationship in his life: that with Sir Alex Ferguson. Fergie was still some way away from reaching breaking point where David was concerned, and, despite his ongoing worries about David's superstar status, the pair remained extremely close. Not that Sir Alex was exactly a cosy figure. 'He frightens the hell out of players but, when you have a manager for so many years, you get used to his ways,' said David. 'The best thing is you know where you stand. If you've done terrible in a game, he'll tell you straight down the line and the next day he'll forget about it. He doesn't hold grudges.'

With the World Cup looming ever closer, David and Victoria seized the chance for a quick trip to visit Sir Elton John in his pink chateau on the Cote d'Azur. The two were becoming accustomed to making headlines practically every time they went outside, but nothing could have prepared them for the fuss occasioned by one of David's new fashion items – a sarong. The two had gone out for dinner à deux at the Chevre D'Or restaurant and, while Victoria, perhaps rather unfortunately, appeared wearing the trousers, David seemed to be wearing a skirt.

That a one-off appearance could strike such a national debate was yet another sign of the phenomenon David was becoming. From here it was just one short step to icon. Except that it wasn't. The World Cup was about to begin – and it was during the tournament that a petty flash of temper very nearly cost David his career.

Indeed, the World Cup was attracting its own fair share of comment before it had even begun. There had already been uproar in some quarters when it emerged that Paul Gascoigne, who sadly had begun that long march downhill in earnest, was not going to play; now there was a second huge fuss when David's team-mate Teddy Sheringham was spotted drinking while out in the Algarve.

David stood up for his team-mate – and, goodness knows, he was going to need some serious support himself before too long. 'It is not my place to make any sort of judgement on Teddy – that is down to the England boss,' he said. 'But what I will say is that, knowing Teddy as I do, I have no doubt he will be up for it at the World Cup. No way, whatever has happened, whatever has been going on, will he not be totally fit and ready. I'm sure the events of the last few days will give him an even greater incentive to prove everyone wrong.'

And so the World Cup finally began. Almost immediately it looked as if it was not going to be a good tournament for David, because he simply wasn't being picked. England's opening match was against Tunisia and, to David's horror, he was dropped in favour of Darren Anderton. It was an awful setback, one that upset not only David, but also Sir Alex Ferguson and Sir Bobby Charlton.

'Alex Ferguson has already said that he was a little disappointed that Glenn Hoddle put David in front of his press corps and I would have to agree with that,' said Sir Bobby. 'David wants to be the best player in the world. He just knows he has so much skill and ability and I don't think he understands why he's not playing. He has an ability which isn't anywhere else in the team. His passing and ability to score goals, the quality of his crossing if he plays on the right side. You're looking at one of the rare players in the world. He's got fantastic ability.'

That was praise indeed from one of the biggest names in football, but it did nothing to cheer David up. His mood began to worsen and his friend Teddy Sheringham was now the one to offer support. 'Yes, David is very down,' he said. 'I was surprised he wasn't chosen, especially as he played in all the eight qualifiers – perhaps it's a sign of all the excellent players we have now.'

As for Hoddle himself, he was very irritable when his judgement was questioned, pointing out that England had won the match 2–0.

David continued to brood. Perhaps it was because he was now the focus of so much attention that being passed over on the pitch wounded him deeply, especially as he knew that he was now a world-class footballer. 'I have had a few days to think about it and I still don't know what went wrong,' he said, a little while after the match. 'The manager did sit down and explain a few things, but it was more of a pat on the back. I did ask him why I wasn't there but I'd rather keep the answer between us. He just sees some things different to me.'

It was a shame that Victoria wasn't there, for she and David might have been able to talk it through. But she was thousands of miles away, touring America with the Spice Girls, and so there was no one, other than his team-mates, that David could really turn to. And the brooding was turning into temper, resulting in an uncharacteristic lashing out when a journalist asked if he hadn't been chosen because he had a difficult personality (for which, read 'was getting big-headed').

'There's people who don't know me as a person and they shouldn't start judging,' he snarled. 'I don't think I have done anything wrong in terms of what happens around me. Stuff goes on because people take pictures of me when I'm out. Just because I've got a famous girlfriend doesn't mean I'm up in the clouds and no one can speak to me. I didn't sulk, like a few people suggested. I didn't say much to the manager. I asked questions and he gave answers, but he did not say I wouldn't be playing again, thank goodness.

'You could argue I wasn't reproducing my usual form and I have heard it said that I dipped. Maybe in a couple of games I was tired but the manager picked me in every one that mattered and I don't think my form has been affected that much. It would have been nice to play for just ten minutes against Tunisia and I think I would have felt better had I got on. But the manager has his team and he sticks with that. In the end there's nothing I can do or say if that's his decision.'

David was clearly feeling deeply resentful and it was eating away at him. Glenn Hoddle, meanwhile, was also feeling resentful, but in his case it was because of the very public criticism levelled at him by Sir Alex Ferguson, and he lashed out at the Manchester United manager in a war of words that was rapidly becoming a sideshow to the World Cup itself. 'David was not focused coming into the tournament – he was vague – and maybe his club need to look at that further,' he remarked. 'I had a chat with him and he's more focused now but I needed to have words before that sank in. I love him to bits – after all, I brought him in. But he's got to understand that football comes first. His focus was not there but now he understands what I'm looking for.'

Nor was he happy about Ferguson's comments about David. 'Everyone is different, but I would never have put that sort of pressure on Alex Ferguson before a big European game,' he said. 'To come out with some of the things he said on the eve of a World Cup game was unprofessional. People can have their own opinions and they are welcome to them. It's a bit disappointing, but it's not just Ferguson doing it – there are other people, on TV and in newspapers.'

The pressure was clearly beginning to tell.

And then, just briefly, everything seemed to get better. First, David was brought on as a substitute in England's second match against Romania and then he played in the next game, a match against Colombia. Here he showed his true worth, scoring a goal with a free kick and thus contributing to the 2–0 win.

Then, quite suddenly – calamity struck.

With David on such good form, it made sense to play him in England's next match, against Argentina, and so he duly ran out on the field with the rest of the team. Then, just over halfway through the match, David was fouled by the Argentine captain Diego Simeone and, in a very petty display of retribution, David clipped him with his heel. Simeone collapsed theatrically to the ground, seemingly in terrible pain. It was a display that, in retrospect, was almost certainly hammed up, but it achieved its purpose and David was shown the red card and sent off, instead of merely receiving the yellow card, which was widely held to be the appropriate punishment for his crime.

From that moment, England's (and David's) fate was sealed. The remaining ten members of the team gave an outstanding performance, but the match ended 2–2, with Argentina winning 4–3 on penalties. England hadn't only lost the match: it had lost the World Cup too. Glenn Hoddle was livid. His former warnings that David had to keep his temper under control had been proven spot on and the consequences of what he had done were immense.

'That cost us dearly,' said a grim–faced Hoddle. 'With ten men, we defended like lions. It's a bitter, bitter pill to take and we are absolutely distraught but proud at the same time. I don't know if it was destiny – everything just went against us. It's not a night for excuses, it's a night for us to be proud for England.'

Hoddle's attitude was completely understandable, but what he had failed to grasp was quite how great the backlash would be against Beckham. Others involved were not surprised. Sir Bobby Charlton, who had been in the game long enough to know exactly how the fans would react, tried to head off the furore that would ensue. 'You cannot throw him to the wolves,' he implored. 'I saw him after the match and he was terribly affected by it. He realised what he had done. I have not seen any replays but David Beckham was brought down and reacted by kicking out, for which he was given a red card.

'That came after England's great first-half performance and it was always going to be difficult against one of the best sides in the world. Everyone knows the consequences of reacting. He's a young lad and he's paid a very high price. I know that, and he will have other World Cups where he can put that right. But it made life difficult for the rest of his team and he appreciates this, too.'

Indeed, David himself was clearly appalled by what he'd done and issued a public apology. 'This is, without doubt, the worst moment of my career and I will always regret what I did,' he said. 'I have apologised to my England team-mates and manager Glenn Hoddle and I want every English supporter to know how sorry I am.'

With that, he flew to New York to be with Victoria, really the only person who could provide comfort at such a terrible time. She too begged the public to be forgiving. 'Please don't hate him,' she said. 'He doesn't deserve to be the most hated man in Britain. He, more than anyone, wanted England to go all the way. I am as upset as everyone in Britain. David needs my support. I just want to be with him. We love each other very much and it is important to get us through this.'

But none of this had any impact whatsoever. England fans and even people who had no interest in football were furious with David and they were determined to make him suffer for what he had done. David was to find himself at the centre of a campaign of vilification the like of which had rarely been seen before.

It started innocuously enough: Adidas, one of David's sponsors, withdrew two advertisements featuring their star, saying they had 'run their course'. Then West Ham supporters had their say. West Ham were to play United in the latter's first away game of the season in August; six weeks before the match, the fans hung a threatening poster at the gates of Upton Park.

But the real campaign of hatred against David was only just getting started. Ted and Sandra Beckham were also receiving abuse and had to be put under police protection. In one of the vilest moments of the persecution of Beckham, an effigy of him was hung up outside the Pleasant Pheasant pub in South Norwood, London. The police eventually insisted it was taken down. Another pub, the Horse and Groom in Islingwood, East Sussex, got in on the act: the owner, Phil Murray, filed a lawsuit against Becks over loss of earnings, claiming takings fell when England were booted out of the World Cup.

By this time, it was becoming clear to some less hot-headed souls in the footballing community that the punishment was far outweighing the crime. Again, proponents of the beautiful game made an effort to defend their young star and to tell the fans that it had gone far enough. Glenn Hoddle himself made a public plea for peace. 'I hope the fans are going to be fair,' he said. 'He's reacted in a foolish way and has to understand that he can't react like that again. Why do we always need a scapegoat? He put in a fantastic performance against Colombia, but all that gets forgotten. David's had to take a bit of stick already in his career and it will be sad if that gets worse because of this, but that's the nature of our game.

'I would plead with people to look at the positive aspect of his games in an England shirt, although he's a strong enough character to take it on the chin. David is very down but we will have a chat and he's got to learn from it. We must not go overboard about it – it's not a time to blame anybody. What David did wasn't violent conduct and it shouldn't have been a red card. Then again, it was such a foolish thing to do and he has to understand he can't do those sorts of things at this level. We've been trying to drum that into him for some time but there's no blame to be put on anybody's shoulders here. He might even become a better player if he goes on to learn from this.'

Perhaps he did, for David has certainly never committed an act of similar idiocy on the field since then. But, despite the constant pleas for restraint and compassion from the game's insiders, it was to be months before David found his way back into the public's favour.

It was a miserable time. David went around dressed all in black, with a black hat covering his hair, clearly trying to look

as inconspicuous as possible. His misery was so apparent that
the golfer Lee Westwood called for him to be left alone. 'It's
sad when the public can't look upon sport as a game,' he said.
'At the end of the day, it is not life and death.'

Training began in mid-July and, for the first time in over
a month, David began to look a little bit more cheerful. He
was caught horsing around on the field with Teddy
Sheringham: the latter pushed Beckham off the ball and
David responded by flicking his right foot at him as a joke.
He even managed a smile. Everyone began to relax a little
and David even began to be able to walk around the streets
near his home again without causing a riot.

It was at this time that a move to Real Madrid was first
suggested. Such was the intensity of the feelings aroused
that many believed David would simply not be able to
continue living in this country. But the fact was that David
didn't want to go – and neither, back then, did Sir Alex
Ferguson wish to lose his brilliant player. David was not,
however, quite up to facing the public yet: he pulled out of
a friendly against Birmingham. His England team-mate
Gareth Southgate, who had himself been the recipient of
venom from the fans when he missed in a penalty shootout
against Germany in the semi-final of Euro 96, warned
David that he would just have to take it.

'The next few weeks are not going to be very nice for
David,' he said. 'The poor lad has already gone through far
more than I ever suffered, but I can still give him some
good advice because of my own experience. I took a lot of
stick, including verbal abuse, nasty letters and people
crossing the road to avoid me. The way you deal with it is
the important thing and I was determined to stand up, be

a man and try to explain to all those critics that football is merely a game.

'Eventually, the tide turned for me. Most people were sympathetic and I am certain this will be the case for David as well. I have every confidence he can win this battle, even though it is going to be hard for him – very, very hard. David seems a quiet lad, yet I have no doubt he possesses the character and personality to come out the other side.'

David must have been enormously heartened by those words and even more so when he played in a friendly in Oslo against part-timers Valerenga. It was his first game for United since the match against Argentina and he was given a hero's welcome, with 20,000 fans roaring their approval as the teams were read out. Even before the match began, the fans were determined to tell David he was out of the wilderness: he was presented with a Player of the Year trophy by the Norwegian branch of the United fan club.

There were still rumblings from some quarters, not least when United played Arsenal at Wembley and rival fans gave David to understand that they had not been pleased with his actions, but they were increasingly muted. United itself could not have been more supportive, not least when, in mid-August, David signed a new five-year £6 million contract with the club. Fears that he might leave the country had been proved wrong. 'I'm delighted to commit myself to the club long-term,' he said. 'This is where I grew up and where I want to stay. It's a great start to the new season for me because it's a special club with some very special players.'

Alex Ferguson also expressed his delight. 'I am really

pleased,' he said. 'This obviously confirms United's intentions to have all of their major players signed on long-term deals. It speaks very highly of our players' commitment to the club and United's commitment to them and their futures.'

The shows of support were becoming increasingly public as David worked – or rather, played – his way back into the nation's heart. United kicked off the season against Leicester City at Old Trafford, resulting in a 2–2 draw, with David scoring one of the goals. The Old Trafford crowd had been vocal in its support, something acknowledged by David as he raised his right fist in tribute. He was publicly embraced on the field both by United's assistant manager Brian Kidd and by Leicester's Robbie Savage, a friend of David's and someone who had played with him in United's Youth team. Savage did, however, warn that it was not over yet. 'I'm afraid this is going to go on for months,' he said. 'David has to go to West Ham next week, when it will be different again. And I suspect that, when United come to Leicester, he'll still be getting some stick.'

Indeed, that first away game at West Ham was seen as something of a potential crisis point for the player. But then, something happened to divert everyone's attention – Victoria revealed that she was three months pregnant. That time in the South of France had clearly proved fruitful and David and Victoria, both of whom were keen to start a family, were thrilled. 'I'm absolutely delighted,' said Victoria. After all the drama of the summer, there could have been nothing better to cheer up David again – and to take his mind off that forthcoming match.

David, however, was still saying nothing publicly. That dreaded West Ham match was finally upon him and a mob of about 500 fans behaved appallingly. David was pelted with stones and hit with a beer glass as the crowd booed and jeered him. And their fury was not solely because of the World Cup: many were enraged that a player from east London should be part of the United team. David behaved magnificently: he rose above it all, said nothing and got on with the game, which resulted in a 0–0 draw.

David continued to redeem himself on the field. Playing against Barcelona in late September, he delivered one of his wonder goals, which drew praise not only from Glenn Hoddle but even Barcelona's goalkeeper, the Dutchman Ruud Hesp. 'I knew where it was going once he struck it, but he has such a brilliant ability in these situations that there was no easy way to get to the ball,' he said. 'If he catches it right, I doubt there is any goalkeeper in the world who can stop him. People might say, if you know where it's going why doesn't the keeper move further over? But, if you go too far, he'd spot that and hit it into the opposite corner.'

But yet more drama was in store. It was not only rogue photographers who were out to cause trouble; 'glamour models' were out to do their bit too. And so it was that one Sunday in October a newspaper ran a shocking story, alleging that David had kissed and flirted with Page 3 girl Emma Ryan and even suggested they get a hotel room, before deciding he couldn't go through with it because of his love for Victoria. It was complete nonsense and the pair laughed it off publicly, although Victoria later wrote in her autobiography about the pain it had caused. It also provoked more claims from another woman that were to prove unfounded.

'There is no way I could have survived the World Cup aftermath without Victoria,' David reflected. 'That's why I went straight to New York to be with her. She didn't say a word when I saw her, just gave me a big cuddle. She was about a month pregnant – no one knew except us – and was as pleased to see me as I was to see her. No way did I expect things to turn as nasty as they did but, once I was with her, I knew I'd get through it.'

Eventful as this year had been, the next was to be equally dramatic. David was to become a father and a husband, in that order, and celebrate a wedding that overshadowed even that of Prince Edward and Sophie Rhys-Jones. But it was not all to be plain sailing for, as David's fame and popularity was to soar ever higher, one man was increasingly dismayed by the turn of events.

4

It was a typical Beckham start to the new year: David celebrated the arrival of 1999 by buying a new £150,000 silver Ferrari 550 Maranello. It was a beautiful car, fit for a famous footballer – although, as onlookers observed, it was a two-seater with nowhere to store the nappies. No matter, David had come through a very difficult year and clearly felt he deserved a little present to cheer himself up.

He was playing well, with no major upsets, but there did seem to be a slight change in his lifestyle. Beckham had always loved clothes and revelled in being a fashion icon but, now more than ever, he seemed to be entering into Victoria's world. The two were pictured and interviewed for *Vogue*, lying entwined around each other and with Victoria's seven-month bump clearly visible.

David went on record to address Glenn Hoddle's accusation, namely that he was not sufficiently focused on the game. 'Personally, I didn't agree with that comment about me not being focused,' he said. 'I've been brought up to believe that, whether you're playing on Hackney Marshes or in the World Cup, you give it everything you've got. My dad, my Sunday league managers – especially one called Stewart Underwood almost 20 years ago – and now Alex Ferguson have always stressed that to me. I don't start focusing when the whistle goes, I start on the Wednesday before Saturday's match or sooner.'

The wounds from that shattering time had clearly not entirely healed. 'It was frustrating not to play in the first two games when I was so keen to do my best for my country,' he went on. 'My feelings never seemed to matter. I want to stress that I'm always happy to respect a manager's wishes but I was very keyed up by the time I got to play and I think things might have turned out differently if I'd played in those two games.' It was the closest David had ever got to blaming Glenn Hoddle for the whole debacle.

David was also keen to clarify his attitude towards his own celebrity. 'I can see how the public or football fans might think I'm letting things slip or getting distracted by celebrity nonsense but what they don't understand is that I can't step out of the front door without getting photographed – and what happens in 10 seconds of my life can stay in the papers for a month,' he said. 'I'm not flash. I like nice things and a nice lifestyle – not because they portray an image to the outside world but because they make me happy. But nothing distracts me from my football.

'I have no great desire to play abroad, but you can never say never,' he said. 'United might get sick of me and sell me abroad or to London, but I want to stay at United for the rest of my career and continue to repay the debt I owe to the boss, the club and the best fans in the world. After that, management holds no appeal for me. What I would really like to do is open a school of excellence for kids – boys and girls. It's not a normal ambition for a footballer but it's something I've always wanted to do. A lot of people helped me to get where I am and I want to put something tangible back into the game.'

As David prepared for fatherhood, there was another ordeal to be faced – Diego Simeone, the player whose antics got David sent off in the World Cup. The two were to meet at Old Trafford when Simeone's team, Inter Milan, came to play in the Champions League and it was a reunion that was expected to be tense. Simeone attempted to extend an olive branch before the match. 'I want to make it known that I respect David Beckham and all of his Manchester United team-mates,' he said. 'I have a lot of admiration for him as a footballer. He is a fantastic player. One of United's greatest strengths is their crosses, and Beckham and Ryan Giggs can pose problems for any fullback. They test the best defences.

'It is not for David Beckham to feel guilty over his sending off at the World Cup and what happened after it. This is football – the same thing has happened to me. The referee believes you have done something wrong and you must go off. I know what has been said but these are the facts: Argentina won the match against England because we beat them in a penalty shootout. That is all, no other reason. Such a thing can not be the fault of one player. As far as I am concerned, our duel is history. That was the World Cup and this is the Champions League and Inter is all that matters to me now.'

David did not reply.

Simeone made matters still worse when he confessed to

overreacting during the match. 'Let's just say the referee fell into the trap,' he told an Italian newspaper. 'It was difficult for him because I went down well and, in moments like that, there's lots of tension. My falling transformed a yellow card into a red card. In reality, it wasn't a violent blow, it was just a little kick back with no force behind it.' These were words that were scarcely likely to endear him to United fans – let alone to David himself.

United beat Inter 2–0, with David setting up Dwight Yorke for the two goals. Alex Ferguson was delighted. 'Beckham is back to his best,' he said. 'They could not handle him or Dwight Yorke. I didn't say anything to David about Simeone before he went out. I didn't need to. I think he is an outstanding central midfield player. But he is also the best crosser of a ball in Europe. And, until I find someone who can cross a ball as well, he will stay out on the right.'

David, meanwhile, was gracious in his triumph. He and Simeone actually embraced and exchanged shirts before David went to acknowledge the rapture from the crowd.

It was a fitting end to the drama and, as if to acknowledge a new beginning, Victoria went into labour the very next day. She was taken to London's Portland Hospital where, on 4 March 1999, she gave birth to a 7lb boy named Brooklyn Joseph Beckham. He was called Brooklyn because that's where Victoria was when she found she was pregnant, while Joseph is both David's middle name and the name of one of his grandfathers.

With his home life so secure, David was beginning to put the events of the past year into perspective. Glenn Hoddle had recently published an account of the World

Cup, in which he revealed that he ignored David after the game, believing it would be best to leave him alone – a decision that David found deeply wounding. 'When I was shown the red card, I was really gutted,' he said. 'More than anything I wanted to play the rest of the game. That was the only thing I was really thinking about – and the team winning, of course.

'I was sat outside the changing room afterwards when Tony Adams came over. He sat down with me and he was brilliant. I will remember that because that was what I needed at the time. The manager didn't actually speak to me after the game. Not at all. My family and friends were the only people who wanted to talk to me.'

But David conceded that he had learned a great deal from the whole experience. 'It made me grow up a lot,' he said. 'It has made me realise a few things, although I feel that with everything that happened after the World Cup I was treated unfairly. I think the majority [of fans] dislike me. I don't know whether it's jealousy or not, but I think there are more people who don't like me than like me. I'd like to be really popular, but I don't think that is going to happen now.'

United beat Chelsea 2–0 a few days later, and while both goals were scored by Dwight Yorke, he paid tribute to David after the first one by making a baby-rocking sign with his arms. Despite David's public comments about the hurt he'd felt at the hands of Glenn Hoddle, the England manager was also generous in his praise. 'He's got good support around him and it's not only good to see him playing excellently, but also that his family life's going well,' he said. 'If people leave him alone, I'm sure he's going to go from strength to strength.'

Ferguson, though, was leaving David in no doubt that he was expected to carry on as usual. Despite admitting to tiredness, he played in all five of United's matches in the two weeks after Brooklyn's birth and by the time the team played Everton in late March, he was beginning to look exhausted. However, he pulled himself together in the second half, scoring a magnificent goal and leading his team on to a 3–1 victory. Even Ferguson was impressed.

Meanwhile, David and Victoria were beginning to prepare for their summer wedding. After months of indecision, the two finally decided to marry in Ireland, at a spectacular venue called Luttrellstown Castle. The venue was just outside Dublin and the ceremony, which was to be covered by *OK!* Magazine in a £1 million deal, was to take place on 4 July, exactly four months after Brooklyn's birth.

Nothing was too much for David to do to show his devotion to his newborn son. He had the name 'Brooklyn' tattooed along the lower half of his back. There was a brief health scare when Victoria discovered a lump in Brooklyn's stomach when she was changing him, but it turned out to be an umbilical hernia that had to be removed. 'It's a routine op and the doctors have said not to worry,' said a spokeswoman for Victoria.

Brooklyn returned to health and with David newly named by *France Football* magazine as the second-highest paid footballer in the world after Ronaldo – he was now estimated to be earning £3 million a year – everything in the garden should have been rosy. But, as ever, there were rumblings of discontent in the background. For a start, rumours continued that Victoria was not happy living in the north and that she wanted David to move to another club. She denied it, but the couple still admitted that their Cheshire home was not permanent and that they were looking to buy a house in the south.

And, as ever, there was the constant worry about David's relationship with Alex Ferguson. Brooklyn's birth had only intensified interest in the couple, on top of which David's publicity was now being looked after by Outside Organisation. These were the Spice Girls' agents and it was at Victoria's behest that David put his business with them. Sir Alex was saying nothing – for now.

5

May arrived – the culmination of a season that had begun with vilification for David but was ending with the promise of unprecedented glory. He celebrated his 24th birthday with a quiet party at the couple's Cheshire home. Shortly afterwards he assured fans for the umpteenth time that he had no plans to quit United. 'I never had any doubts about staying,' he said. 'I think, at the start of the season, a lot of people were wondering whether I would crack. Or whether I would go abroad. But all I wanted was to come back to United and to be playing again.

'At times it has been hard getting that reaction from the crowds, but the lads here have been brilliant for me. I couldn't have asked for more support. And I never had any doubts about staying. I knew I was going to get stick when I went to away grounds. I've had that every away game. But I'm playing for the biggest club in the world so I expect that. You learn as you go along and it makes you a much stronger person.'

As David shared Victoria's excitement over their wedding, his football career was coming to a head. United were chasing hard for the Premiership title, and had made it through to the final of both the FA Cup and the Champions League. No club had ever won all three in the same season. And the papers were getting excited about Becks the footballer again.

'One minute they wanna hang you, the next you're gonna win the game against Luxembourg – my "comeback game",' he reflected ruefully. 'There's never been a point where I thought, "Right, I've won them over," because I don't think I ever will. The papers are probably writing nicer things about me, but there's still time in my career for them to change their minds again!'

United clinched the Premiership title, then won the FA Cup Final against Newcastle, with Ferguson singling out David for praise. And when they beat Bayern Munich in a nail-biting Champions League final in Barcelona on 26 May, their place in history was secured. The team was now being spoken of as one of the greatest ever, with Beckham in particular increasingly being cited as a truly great footballer.

Cradling the Champions Cup after the Bayern Munich match, David yet again vowed his loyalty to Manchester United, not least because he knew he was an increasingly attractive proposition to other European clubs. 'I always want to be a Manchester United player, of course I do,' he said exultantly. 'When you do things like winning the European Cup, why would you want anything else? Why go anywhere else? It couldn't possibly get better wherever I went.'

The subject of Beckham's best position had been a regular topic of debate. His brilliant crossing made him a natural choice for the right of midfield, but his vision, passing and workrate were well suited to a central role – one that Becks himself was said to prefer. Indeed, he had played there against Bayern Munich, in the absence of the suspended Roy Keane and Paul Scholes, and had been instrumental in United's goals with his dead ball delivery. But he wasn't being drawn into the debate.

'I'll play whatever position the manager wants me to. I have no problem with that – whether it's the centre or wide right.' And he reflected on an ultimately satisfying season. 'It's been a tough season of hard work, but when you end up with three trophies, as we have, you know all the hard work has been worth it. You can't better it, of course, but you can repeat it and this win gives us the incentive to go on and look to the future because we want to win all three again.'

The question had been not whether Sir Alex would sell David, but whether Beckham would leave of his own accord. And David wanted to make it absolutely clear where his loyalties lay. The only problem – in Ferguson's eyes if in no one else's – was that he had another life, a very different life, in the south of England. And Sir Alex was beginning to think that perhaps the two would not mix.

But others were not so concerned. New England boss Kevin Keegan said, 'We've got a lot of captains in the side and David has shown true leadership qualities recently. We all saw them against Bayern Munich.' It was a hint of more glories to come.

'At the moment, everything is perfect,' David said. 'That's a nice feeling to have. We've won the treble, I'm in the England squad, playing regularly – and, of course, my private life is perfect, too, with my new little boy.'

The wedding was now less than a month away and David and Victoria were spotted carrying on business as usual: they were pictured going shopping in London's Knightsbridge – with David flashing the cash as much as his bride-to-be.

Beckham's parents were understandably delighted with all the praise and good fortune being heaped on their talented boy. Ted was asked if he'd felt let down by David's actions in the previous year's World Cup. 'No, not at all – it's only a game of football, after all – but I know that David felt he'd let his team-mates down,' he said. 'After the game, we went up to him and cuddled him. I think he was upset for the older players, because he knew they wouldn't get another chance to play in the World Cup. Everybody was upset with David, but to slaughter a player like the press did is beyond me. More could have been done to protect him.'

Ted went on to recall the time when David first became interested in football. 'I've always been a big football fan and a Manchester United supporter,' he said. 'As a young man I played football for Leyton Orient and Walthamstow. I used to run a Sunday league side and David used to come with me from the age of four or five. When the game was over, he and I would practise on the pitch together, kicking and shooting till half past ten or eleven o'clock at night. I knew he was good. He had things I'd never seen in a little kid before – he had crossing ability and control. He never said he wanted to be anything else other than a footballer, and he always said that one day he was going to play for Manchester United.'

David was clearly destined to be a footballer right from

the outset. Sandra went on to reveal more about David's abilities when he was little more than a toddler. 'We used to take lots of cine-films when David was little and in every one he's got a ball,' she said. 'We've got a film of him at 18 months, wearing a little Manchester United strip. We've kept all his United kits since then. From the age of seven, he used to play in the park across the road, where I knew he'd be safe. I had a friend who worked in the hut there, and I used to ring and tell her he was on his way so she could keep an eye on him.

'As a child, David was quite short for his age,' added Sandra. 'When he went to Manchester United at the age of 16, he was smaller than me. I'm five foot four.' 'He shot up the following year,' said Ted. 'They must've put him in a growbag! I remember going to see him in Manchester and talking to Nobby Stiles. He used to say to me, "Don't worry, Mr Beckham, he'll be six foot one day." And he was right!'

Above: David Beckham joins Manchester United on the day of his 14th birthday. His family and Alex Ferguson stand in the background.

Below: Young but already powerful – Beckham in flight.

Above left: David with Eric Cantona. At this time, David was lodging with Annie and Tommy Kay in Manchester.

Above right: The Kay's house where David lived between the ages of 16 and 21.

Below: Beckham making his league debut for Manchester United against Leeds United.

David Beckham's was a swift rise – here he is seen carrying the 1997 P.F.A. Young Player of the Year cup.

There's only one David Beckham! David celebrates scoring for
England in the 1998 World Cup against Colombia.

Above: The man in action. Yet another Beckham goal, this time against Chelsea.

Below left: The perfect gentleman off the pitch, David's passionate relationship with football has sometimes got him in trouble whilst on the grass. Here he vents his frustration at referee Gerald Ashby during a match against Leicester City.

Below right: Five great footballers (*from left*): Ryan Giggs, Denis Irwin, Teddy Sheringham, David Beckham and Andy Cole, all in the famous Manchester United red.

David Beckham after the final whistle for Manchester United vs. Real Madrid in the UEFA Champions League.

Above: Another goal for Beckham; this time against Finland.

Below: Becks receives the captain's armband from coach Peter Taylor.

Above left: David and Victoria at The Winter Wonderland ice rink in Hyde Park, December 2007.

Above right: David training with LA Galaxy.

Below: Although the Beckhams now live in the States, David will always be considered a national treasure in this country. He was one of a select few stars that Michael Parkinson personally chose to appear on his final show.

6

By the start of the new millennium, David and Victoria had been married for over six months and David's fame had grown so great that he was now the subject of security scares. United were due to fly to Brazil in early January to play in the World Club Championships and there were real fears that they might be the subject of a kidnapping attempt. In total, the club's players were worth at least £100 million, with David alone accounting for £30 million of that. The Brazilians were ordered to step up security. 'We have done everything we can to minimise the risk to the team,' said Rio police chief Major Marinho. 'We don't expect problems, but there is always the possibility of one.'

The team headed for Rio, with an anxious Victoria telling David to be careful. She had also repeated her comment in an interview to the effect that David wore her underpants, resulting in a further flurry of newspaper headlines. David had other things to worry about: in the opening game of the World Club Championship in Rio he was sent off during the team's first game against the Mexican side Necaxa. Fergie – who had also been told to leave the 'technical area' following a row with a FIFA official – was supportive. 'The Mexican players got David sent off,' he said, while dismissing his own contretemps – and the match ended in a 1–1 draw.

All of that was completely overshadowed when a Sunday newspaper ran a story claiming that there was indeed a kidnap plot – but it involved Victoria and Brooklyn, not David. Although it later turned out that the paper had paid £10,000 for a story without much foundation, it caused serious alarm, and the couple immediately arranged for increased security at all times.

The circus surrounding the family just continued to grow. Kevin Keegan, the England manager, attempted to defuse some of the pressure when he said, 'To me, David Beckham is not a celebrity but a tremendously talented player – and that's all I'm interested in. In the back of my mind I know there are other things that come with him, with Michael Owen and with Alan Shearer. But they're not celebrities when they're with England. The problem people like David face is that everybody is trying to get a piece of the action because the media is a monster, which needs feeding constantly.

'But I've never seen any indication that the pressure is getting to David. He mixes well with all the boys. Whenever he comes in to the England squad he's a model player, and I've never had any problems with him. He's a winner and it goes without saying he's a tremendous player. The judgement on David now, though, is either a positive or a negative – there's nothing in between. He's either at the top of the sky or down in the pits, but as a manager I try to go along a middle line.'

United were certainly only too keen to hang on to David at that time. His pay was inching ever higher, now at around the £60,000-a-week mark as the club sought to fend off interested rivals. And it was David's father, of all people, who hinted that, if the couple continued to be on the receiving end of unkind treatment, then they might pack up and go abroad. 'What has been going on is an absolute disgrace,' he said. 'I think it is a shame because he's just a footballer, after all, and the media are trying to make him into something he isn't. He won't want to leave England but anything is possible at the end of the day.' When the day finally came, of course, it was not the media who pushed David abroad. But at that stage no one dreamed of the rift that was to develop between David and Sir Alex.

At the end of January, United beat Middlesbrough 1–0, with David scoring a goal in the 88th minute, his first of the Premiership season. Football commentators were forecasting that his game could only get better: it was a much-needed boost after the public relations fiasco in Rio.

But given the intensification of media interest since his marriage to Victoria, David was again under the eagle eye of Sir Alex, and the boss didn't like what he saw. The two were involved in a furious row during training in February, when the United manager accused David of spending time in London the previous day when he should have been training. The row got so intense that David finally threw his gloves away and stormed off United's new training ground in Carrington. He was later seen driving away in his black Range Rover, again fuelling speculation that he might be prepared to leave the club.

And, indeed, the situation promptly got worse. It emerged that David's absence had been caused by a health scare involving Brooklyn. The 11 month old boy became ill during the night, prompting Victoria to phone a doctor at 3am. The doctor diagnosed gastroenteritis. Wanting to stay home and care for his son, David phoned in to say he couldn't make training.

But in Ferguson's eyes this was not the way a footballer should behave and the sin was compounded by the fact that David was in Hertfordshire, not Cheshire. David was dropped from the forthcoming match against Leeds United and, not even picked for the substitutes' bench, was forced to watch the match from the stands.

'I picked the team for today and that's it,' said Sir Alex. 'In this situation I didn't pick David. What happened is just one of those things. What we do is inside the club and all things will be dealt with by the club.'

It didn't help that Victoria had been photographed at the British Fashion Awards ceremony on the night that David missed training, albeit without her spouse in tow. But it was the first really serious clash between player and manager since the wedding and many took it to be a sign of the increasing hold Victoria had over her husband. Now she and Ferguson had entered into a battle with one another for David's heart and soul and, right from the start, it was obvious who was going to win – Victoria. But when that finally happened, David would have to go.

Kevin Keegan stepped in to play peacemaker. He picked David to play midfield against Argentina – and no one missed the significance of that – when England played in a friendly. 'What happened at Leeds is a Manchester United thing and only two people can sort that out,' he said. 'As far as I am concerned, David is fit and raring to go, as enthusiastic as ever, and was the last one off the training field as usual.

'I put my trust in him because to me he's just a footballer. People talk about the other things going on in his life and they underestimate him because they don't know him. People pick up the bits and build an image, which I don't think is the guy.' The game ended in a 0–0 draw, but Beckham put in a good performance and for now, at least, the ructions died down.

David spoke publicly about the spat. 'It disappoints me that a little argument between me and the manager was blown up out of all proportion,' he said. 'I felt I had a good reason to miss training. Brooklyn was ill with gastroenteritis. I rang the club and told them that. In the end I abided by what the manager and the club decided and accepted their disciplinary action. I have heard it said I'm trying to be bigger than the club. I'm not and never could be. Nobody can be bigger than the biggest club in the world.

'My relationship with the manager is fine. Players sometimes have bust-ups with their managers but it doesn't mean they have to fall out permanently. With our manager, you can have an argument with him one day and it will be forgotten the next. He's had his say and I've had mine. He's never mentioned it to me since and he doesn't bear grudges.'

Ferguson confirmed that it was all in the past. 'I have had a chat with David. All we can say about him now is that the matter is cleared. It's over. It was finished on the day it began. I hope David is now saying the same positive things about the situation.'

He certainly was. Keen to ensure his loyalty to the club and smooth over any tensions between his wife and his manager, David could scarcely have been more positive. 'I love Manchester United with a passion,' he said. 'It's the only club I ever wanted to play for and I still do. Victoria doesn't want anything to affect that. She has never had a fallout with the manager. She respects him. People are trying to create a rift between them, but I can tell you, it doesn't exist.'

If that were not enough, David went on to talk about Victoria's feelings about Manchester. 'People seem to have this idea that I commute to work between London and Manchester every day. It's nonsense. We have an apartment in Alderley Edge and that is our home. It's where Victoria, Brooklyn and I live. We've bought a house down south and we'll probably live there eventually because that's where we both come from. But that is way in the future.'

The message could not have been clearer. Everything in the garden was rosy and David had absolutely no intention of leaving Man U.

Despite the sudden outbreak of peace, though, David had no intention of adopting a lower profile. And so it was that startled fans saw a sharply crew-cut David run out on to the pitch when United played Leicester, having spent £300 having his locks trimmed. Any bemusement Sir Alex might have felt – and he almost certainly did – would have been allayed by the outcome of the match at least: United won 2–0, with one of the goals scored by Beckham. To celebrate, Brooklyn was given a similar cut.

Trivial as it was, David's haircut made both the front pages and the comment pages of the papers, with speculation rife about why he'd done it and whether he would lose his Brylcreem sponsorship. It was extraordinary that a man, and a footballer, to boot, should attract such attention merely over his appearance, but the public simply could not get enough of Posh and Becks. Every move the two of them made was reported on and every time they changed their partings there was saturation coverage. There was also a rumour that someone had been combing through the hair salon's rubbish bins to get their hands on David's shorn locks.

United continued to go from strength to strength, receiving the Premier League trophy in May. David shaved his head especially for the occasion and took Brooklyn on to the pitch. Roy Keane and Raymond van der Gouw also brought their own children on to the field, while Sir Alex cradled his grandson Jake.

With Euro 2000 next in the calendar, attention turned back to playing for England. Kevin Keegan again voiced his support for the young star. 'Beckham can have a bigger influence on the England set-up than he has had already,' he said. 'I'm not scared to tell him because he knows that as well. There is no limit to how good he can become. He is still young, yet very experienced. Whatever he wants to be, he can be. There's so much more in him.'

Keegan was not alone in that opinion. Brazil ace Roberto Carlos told his team-mates that the best way to ensure a victory is this: stop Beckham. 'Beckham is England's main player,' he said. 'Every time they have the ball, they look to get it to him. If he gets time and space to cross he will cause any team in the world problems.' He was even voted second-best footballer in the world after Brazilian Rivaldo.

David and Victoria took a short break in the States with Brooklyn before David reappeared, looking refreshed and ready for the trials ahead. Everyone was forecasting that he could be the best footballer in the world and now he seemed determined to make it happen. 'I've never felt better in my life,' he said. 'I've got bags of confidence right now. I've come off a good season, won another trophy and I've started to score goals. Now I want to dominate games for England more than I do. I really feel ready.'

England got off to a flyer at Euro 2000, going 2–0 against a much fancied Portugal in just 18 minutes, as Scholes and Steve McManaman got on the end of two trademark Beckham crosses. But by half time Portugal had levelled the score and went on to win 3–2. As David left the pitch, he received such a volley of abuse from a section of the England fans that he ended up giving them a one-fingered gesture.

Kevin Keegan was staunchly supportive. 'I'd have thumped them,' he declared angrily. 'It was the worst thing I've seen in football. I've taken plenty of abuse in my time but this was way beyond anything I've heard. It was very personal. If you'd heard that abuse, if your sons and daughters had to listen to that, you'd have reacted in the same way.'

The entire nation felt the way Keegan did and rallied to David's defence. David responded brilliantly and went on the attack: the second game went far better, with England beating Germany 1–0. This time he walked off the field to cheering. And when, a few days later, England lost 3–2 to Romania and crashed out of the tournament, David was singled out for applause as he left the field.

For the first time, speculation began to mount that David might captain England. Alan Shearer was retiring and, although Keegan had been talking of Tony Adams as his replacement, Adams had not played as well as Beckham in the previous matches and was no longer considered a sure thing.

'I have a great deal of pride when I pull on an England shirt but to captain my country would be the ultimate dream for me,' said David. 'I have always harboured dreams of captaining the teams I play for, be they Manchester United or England, and I can think of no greater honour.'

Despite England's overall performance in Euro 2000, David had emerged with credit and was again being wooed by various rival clubs. AC Milan had approached Sir Alex to ask if he was for sale: the answer was no. At that time Sir Alex wouldn't hear of it and his decision was final.

But then, to everyone's surprise, Sir Alex risked reopening old wounds on the publication of an updated version of his autobiography. He had written about the furious argument he'd had with David earlier in the year, which led to him dropping Beckham for the match with Leeds. 'It doesn't matter to me how high a player's profile is,' he wrote. 'If he is in the wrong, he is disciplined. And David was definitely in the wrong.' It emerged he was particularly angry that Victoria had ventured out while David stayed at home. 'I had to think that David wasn't being fair to his team-mates,' he went on. 'I had to imagine how they would feel if David could adjust the schedule to suit himself. There was no way I could consider including Beckham in the team to meet Leeds. That much was crystal clear in my mind before David worsened the problems between us when we met on the Saturday by making me lose my temper badly, something I hadn't done in years. At first he simply refused to accept he had anything to answer for and that made me blow up.'

One result of that, at least, was to bring out the predators from rival teams who still wanted to get their hands on David. 'I note with interest that Sir Alex Ferguson and David Beckham seem to have a difference of opinion that has not gone away,' commented Joan Gaspart, the newly elected president of Barcelona. AC Milan, having tried at least twice that summer to buy David, also pricked up its ears.

Martin Edwards, chairman of United, stepped in to quash rumours about both David and his team-mate Paul Scholes. 'There is no way we would allow them to go,' he snapped. 'They are the backbone of this team and we want them to remain at United. We would be extremely reluctant to see either player leave.'

David maintained a diplomatic silence. He could afford to. Just for once it seemed that Fergie was unwise, to put it mildly, to bring up that row again, especially after both had gone to such lengths to publicly avow it was all over.

7

As the new football season approached, there was a noticeable change in the fans' attitude. There was a sense that they had gone too far during Euro 2000 and almost seemed to be trying to make it up to him. At a pre-season match in York, the fans actually cheered him as he ran out on to the pitch, much to David's own bemusement. 'It was nice to get a good reception at York,' he said. 'In pre-season last year I was getting booed here and there, but it made a nice change at the weekend.'

David's new-found popularity went straight to his pocket. Well aware that rival clubs would grab him the moment they could, it was rumoured that United offered to raise his pay packet to £80,000 a week. 'David will be here for as long as I'm manager,' said Ferguson with typical managerial hyperbole. 'He's not pushing for any new negotiations on his contract and he's looking forward to the new season.' But he did hint that there might be a pay rise at the end of the season.

Kevin Keegan helped matters further when he hinted that David could become England captain. 'He might not be the most vocal of players but he's got leadership qualities.'

There were the usual rumours about the possibility of his moving abroad, the usual round of denials from everyone and then, in October, the publication of *Beckham: My World*, a sort of coffee-table picture book, which contained a few telling insights. David revealed that he would love to go skiing when he eventually stops playing football as he can't currently do so because of the insurance, and that he would love to fly to the moon one day, were it ever possible.

He also talked about building a football pitch at the new home in Hertfordshire and having horses. 'The new house is perfect for a five-a-side pitch for me and Brooklyn,' he wrote. 'I'd like us to have three or four more babies. That would keep me busy.' And there was every chance that they would do so, given that he went on to write, 'I'm often asked whether scoring a goal is better than sex. For me there is no contest. Of course, sex is better.'

And, of course, the book was a best-seller. As the hostility created by the 1998 match against Argentina died away, it was replaced by straightforward hero worship. David turned up at Manchester's Trafford Centre for a book signing, where he was mobbed by a crowd of thousands.

In October a dream also came true: David was named as England captain as they prepared to play a friendly against Italy in Turin. 'This is one of the proudest moments in my footballing career,' he said. 'When I was a kid, I used to dream about leading England out.'

England coach Peter Taylor, in charge for just this

match, was in no doubt that Beckham was the right man for the job. 'He deserves to be captain,' he said. 'He'll take the responsibility on board, he'll respond to it and I hope in the right way. He has matured greatly since the 1998 World Cup. He is a marvellous player and I think he will handle the responsibility of leading the team. He looks like he desperately wants to play for Manchester United and England, that he loves his football and I intended to give him the captaincy from the moment the FA asked me to take charge for this one-off game. All the other players respect David and I see no reason why he can't go on and captain England for many years to come.'

David took his new responsibilities seriously. 'I won't stand up and give a speech but it's my job to go up to players and talk to them,' he said. 'I'm not used to doing that because I'm quite shy. It'll be hard for me but I've got to learn to do things like this and I'm sure I'll do it. It's exciting because everyone's talking about the new era – it's great for me to be captain and to lead the team out. I've been quieter than some of the other captains – I won't be shouting. But I can give different things to the team.'

David was also looking forward to playing in midfield. 'I've got to change my game and talk to other players but hopefully I'll be able to do that,' he said. 'I'm pleased I'm playing in the centre as a captain because it'll give me more of a chance to speak to players a bit more and keep the team going. I know everyone will give 110 per cent – but to get a good result over here is really hard.'

It was the fulfilment of a dream, but as yet it was unclear how long David would be England captain. It had just been announced that Sven-Goran Eriksson was to be the new

England manager and his thoughts about the captaincy were as yet unknown.

With an eye on keeping his club and national team managers happy, David was prepared to rein in his new celebrity lifestyle to a certain extent, but he was growing increasingly used to the trappings of fame. And putting his fame to good use. As Christmas approached, the couple visited Christie Hospital in Manchester, where they spent an hour distributing presents to children. It was an extremely generous gesture.

'The youngsters were thrilled,' said a spokesman for the Youth Oncology Unit. 'It's something they will never forget. David and Victoria asked for the visit to be kept quiet. They didn't want any publicity, but they made everyone's Christmas.'

David remained popular elsewhere too. Barcelona popped up again, offering David a deal worth £100,000 a week. Ryan Giggs, Andy Cole, Dwight Yorke and Jaap Stam were also seen as potential defectors to other clubs. Sir Alex wasn't having any of it. 'I would put my life on them staying, as long as we look after them,' he said. 'Nothing is certain in life, but I don't think they want to leave Old Trafford. The important thing is to be top of the league on 1 January. If we are, we will be delighted.'

In the new year, negotiations began over a new contract, with David reportedly turning down an opening offer of £80,000 a week. Under Victoria's guidance, it was believed that David was determined not just to achieve pay parity with his team-mates, but to be paid better than the rest of them. Not everyone was thrilled that Victoria was involved in negotiations, not least the former Nottingham Forest boss Brian Clough, another manager of the old school. 'I'm watching David Beckham with great interest these days,' he said. 'I think he's at a personal crossroads where his great talent and professionalism may collide with his lifestyle. Beckham is a highly talented player who plays for the team and Alex Ferguson has done a brilliant job with him. When necessary he has cracked down on him and Beckham has juggled all the social balls well.'

Clough's advice? 'He should sign a new, long contract with United, persuade his missus to have a few more bairns and get as much rest as he can. And, while he's at it, he should guide Posh in the direction of a singing coach, because she's nowhere near as good at her job as her husband is at his. I used to like my players to marry young, but I had no time for wives who interfered with the football – it was up to my players to control their wives. Alex Ferguson is just as old-fashioned as I am about that.'

In retrospect, reading those words, a clash between Beckham and Ferguson was inevitable. It wasn't just the differing personalities and lifestyles of the two men, it was a generational sea change. Telling Victoria to keep quiet and keep her nose out of it was as useful as telling water to run uphill. It just wasn't going to happen.

8

As Sven-Goran Eriksson moved in as the new England manager, speculation intensified as to whether he would keep David on as captain. Some of the other players had reservations, thinking that, at 25, David was still too young for the job. Eriksson went to Manchester to watch United play early in the year, but ironically David had been given a rest day and was attending a music awards ceremony in the South of France. Eriksson was unperturbed.

'I knew on Friday that David would not be playing but it doesn't matter because as a player I know him,' he said. 'And it doesn't surprise me that he is being rested. Manchester United want to win the Champions League, the Premiership and the FA Cup, and it is impossible for one player to play in all 60 or 70 games. You have to do these things. Alex Ferguson told me a couple of seasons ago that things like this are one of the secrets of United's success.'

He was guarded, though, as to whether David would retain the role of captain. 'I don't know about that. I will wait until I get all the players together,' he said. 'I haven't spoken to David yet or any of the players.'

The speculation did nothing to dent David's popularity. He signed another sponsorship deal, this time with Police sunglasses, worth £1 million, and promptly splashed out on a £185,000 Lamborghini Diablo GT, adding to an already extensive collection. (In later years Sir Elton John was heard to remark, 'I keep telling David, buy paintings, not cars.') He then returned to the football field, helping United to a 6–1 win against Arsenal, prompting more comment about being England's most gifted footballer.

Meanwhile, England's most gifted manager – Sir Alex – was preparing for retirement. 'It's impossible for anyone to try to influence Sir Alex, but I certainly want him to stay,' David said. 'You only have to look at his track record to know what he has done for Manchester United and what a loss he will be when he eventually quits.'

David got his wish – Sir Alex did stay on. Had he not, David might well still be at United today.

Eriksson named David as England captain for the new manager's first game in charge, against Spain at Villa Park. Victoria, who could be seen wiping back tears, was in the crowd, holding Brooklyn as England won 3–0.

'I was so proud of David because I know how much this means to him,' she said. 'It's the greatest honour to captain your country.'

Of course, David was pleased, too, not least because the score gave the new England manager a very good reason for keeping him on as captain. He had been substituted at half-time, but the cool-as-ice Swede manager reassured everyone, that that had been planned all along.

Slightly unsurprisingly, given his much-publicised adoration of his son, David was voted 'Perfect Dad' in a nationwide poll, beating Prime Minister Tony Blair, Bob Geldof, Fatboy Slim and Michael Douglas. But David was feeling jaded. Sir Alex, expressing concern that he might be losing his form, gave him the weekend off, prompting the usual speculation that this might be the end of his time with United. But, while he was resting from United, he was still playing for England and led the team out at Anfield against Finland. England won 2–1, with David scoring the deciding goal. It was a brilliant performance and he was cheered off the pitch – unusual for a United player at Anfield.

'You look at David and he leads by example,' said England team-mate Michael Owen. 'It's important to have a captain who can perform like that.' More importantly still, it silenced the doubters who had wondered whether Eriksson was right to keep Beckham on as captain. His future now seemed assured.

David's friend and team-mate Gary Neville was also delighted and forecast that David would now captain England for some years to come. 'He's more assured and it's a necessity when you're made the England captain,' he said. 'All of a sudden you've got to take on more responsibility and it's not a problem for him. At 26 he's seen most things in football. There's not a lot that he's not seen: World Cups, European Championships, massive games for United. Sometimes at 25 or 26 you need that extra challenge, that extra motivation. Giving him the England captaincy will certainly have given him that and he can be England captain for years to come.'

It was a total, unqualified triumph for David, although he soon learned that, while Liverpool fans might cheer him on for England, it was a different story when he was playing for United. Just one week later he was back at Anfield and, while it was the first time he had played with United for some weeks now, it was not an auspicious occasion. The team lost 2–0, and taunts against Victoria were heard in the crowd. A week turned out to be a long time in football.

David was not unduly concerned: he had now officially attained the status of national hero. But tensions with his boss surfaced again after Sir Alex banned him from attending a charity awards ceremony in London with Victoria. He had been due to pick up the Sports Personality of the Year Award at the Capital FM Help A London Child appeal until Ferguson told him it was impossible to take time off at this stage of the season – despite the fact that he wasn't playing in the next two United matches.

He did, however, make it to London for Victoria's 27th birthday at the end of April a couple of weeks later. And he celebrated his 26th birthday in trademark style: he had a new hairdo, this time a close crop on top of the head and shaved on either side. It was known as a 'step' cut and closely resembled the American GI style. Victoria, meanwhile, gave him a new pair of diamond earrings – David obligingly posed for photographers while wearing them – and the usual furore over his new appearance began.

David was a little bit taken aback by the latest fuss, asking one journalist who kept on about it, 'Do you fancy me or something?' The response was negative, but he was still asked if the style was right for an England captain. 'I don't think it matters,' he said. 'Being England captain is not about the way you look or what you do. I'm not doing it to create attention. Sir Alex was fine and so, too, was

Sven-Goran Eriksson. I don't think he can believe how much is being made of it. He said, if it was your right foot that was the problem, it would be different.'

And, at last, David's people sat down to work out a new contract with United. He was in no hurry to get anything resolved, not least because it was still not clear whether Ferguson would be staying on as manager. There was also the added factor that David was now worth a lot of money to United. They could choose to sell him now, if they wished, for an estimated £30 million whereas, if they waited until his old contract expired, he could walk away and they would get nothing. If they wanted to keep him, therefore, it was in their interests to get him signed up.

David was asked if he wanted to know what the situation was before deciding anything. 'Yes,' David replied, 'and as I've said already there is no rush to sign a new contract. If the club did want to sell me, that would hurt. I love Manchester United. I have been here for 10 years and I have been a supporter of the club all my life. You can never say never about playing abroad, but right now United is where I want to be.'

An added complication for United was that the club now had more people to deal with: Tony Stephens, David's long-term agent, and members of the Outside Organisation who represented Victoria and, at her instigation now had David on their books, too. Again, it led to some concern over the influence Victoria was having over her husband's career – but, as long as David wanted it that way, there was not a great deal anyone could do.

And he continued to model for magazines. His latest appearance was on the cover of The Face, in which he appeared to be spattered with blood (it was actually soy sauce). He then suffered a real injury – a groin strain in a match against Aston Villa – after which it was feared that he would not be able to play in the crucial World Cup qualifier against Germany in Munich. This put David in such a black mood that he couldn't even speak to his father during a two-and-a-half-hour car journey, while Victoria had to endure a week of gloom. In the event, he was able to play, but felt he'd behaved so badly to everyone that he even apologised publicly. 'I was really down after the game, I couldn't speak to anyone,' he said. 'I don't think Victoria has seen me in this sort of mood before. I'm in a mood when we lose but I'm terrible when I'm injured. I'm saying sorry to her now. It has been difficult.'

To everyone's utter delight, England beat Germany 5–1, an outstanding result and England's biggest ever win over Germany. David didn't score any of the goals – Michael Owen, in a game he'll always remember, scored three – but played beautifully, again justifying Eriksson's decision to keep him on as captain.

David was in typically generous form. 'Everyone showed great character after we went a goal down so early on,' he said. 'We just tried to get the ball to Michael Owen and Stevie Gerrard as much as we could.'

As the scale of the victory began to sink in, it was hailed as a victory for England that was second only to the 1966 World Cup. And David had been the captain. When the team went to change after the match, they felt as bemused as everyone else. 'We sat in the dressing room afterwards just looking at each other as if to ask, "What happened there, then?"' David revealed. 'When the world looks at the scoreline, they will be as amazed as we are.' David also said that Eriksson had offered to substitute him before the end because of that groin strain. 'Who would want to miss out on the finish of a night like that?' he asked. 'The moment I will remember most is walking over to the England fans at the end to celebrate. It was an amazing feeling. As the goals started to go in, we kept looking around at each other like we were all thinking, "What the hell is going on?" You could see it on the faces.'

But although the team were allowed a night of celebrations, the next morning it was back to England and straight back to training. Sven-Goran Eriksson might have been ice to Sir Alex Ferguson's fire, but both had exactly the same attitude when it came to keeping their teams ready and fit.

Eriksson realised there was still some way to go to qualify for the World Cup. Germany was still top of the group, with England three points behind, which meant the forthcoming matches against Albania and Greece were crucial. David was well aware of this too. 'The whole nation was behind us in Germany and will be behind us in Newcastle,' he said. 'There'll be no problem about lifting the players for the Albania game, but people need to be patient. Remember it took us more than 70 minutes to score in Albania and their defence could again cause us some problems.'

In a television interview with chat-show host Michael Parkinson, Victoria revealed that she calls her husband 'Goldenballs' – and David proved that he deserved it a week later when England played Greece. Needing only a draw to qualify, the team as a whole were lacklustre and, disastrously, were trailing 2–1 with only seconds left on the clock. With one of his trademark free kicks, David, who had put in a particularly energetic performance, saved the day with an immaculate strike into the corner of the Greek net. 'It's the best feeling ever,' David said after the game. 'We didn't play the prettiest football but for a young team to come back from 1–0 to 1–1, to go 2–1 behind and then come back to 2–2 again, it shows the character of the team and how much we all wanted it. It was a good time to score and one that had to go in.' Beckham's character was shining through on the pitch and in the post-match interview.

Eriksson was glowing about his skipper. 'He played one of the best games I have seen him play. He ran all over the pitch. He was a big captain and if we want to do well in the World Cup, we must do that again. He did everything today to push the team. That was the first step to something that could be very beautiful. Let's be happy today, tomorrow let's try to be better.'

It was hardly surprising that the jubilant David went on to say that he wanted to play in every game he could. Sir Alex wanted to rest him during United's forthcoming match against Olympiakos, but David persuaded him otherwise. 'I don't want a rest, particularly when things are going so well,' he said. However, Fergie did manage to get Beckham to take a weekend off, which he spent jetting to see Victoria, who was now in Scandinavia. And who can blame him for such over-excitement? To go from villain to national treasure – there were even calls for him to be knighted – would please anyone and David, a modest and emotional man, found it especially overwhelming.

9

As Christmas approached, Manchester United had still not come to an agreement with David over his contract. This was becoming a real problem. Christmas had been set as an informal deadline and, if a deal were not sorted out by then, there was a real possibility that United would sell David the following summer, when he had a year left to run. For a start, there was disagreement about the money involved and, on top of that, his representatives favoured a mere two-year extension. United sources claimed that they were near to fixing terms but, interestingly, David had actually started asking colleagues about life abroad. It seems that, as far back as the end of 2001, he was beginning to realise where his future might lie.

But he was still England captain and as such he had responsibilities to pursue – sartorial ones. Much to the amusement of onlookers, Sven-Goran Eriksson had asked him to dress the England side for the World Cup, prompting much ribaldry about sarongs. David responded with dignity. 'It's my job as England captain to organise

things like the suits and pick the colour and style of them,'
he announced. 'Normally the manager has a say but Mr
Eriksson said, "Let him do it."'

David was named BBC Sports Personality of the Year
for 2001 and, dressed as a Chicago gangster, dutifully
thanked his family, Sir Alex, Eriksson and, of course,
Victoria and Brooklyn. It was a generous gesture. David
had again been dropped from the United line-up against
West Ham – and United had lost. There had been some
muttering that, had David been included, the outcome
would have been different, but no one was in the mood to
spark yet another public row. In fact, David went on to say
that Fergie had been right to drop him.

The very next day, David won another award: Britain's
Best-Dressed Man. Shortly after that, he was runner-up for
the FIFA World Player of the Year awards for the second
time in three years, losing narrowly to Real Madrid's Luis
Figo. But still the rumblings of discontent went on. Despite
his public statement, he was said to be increasingly angry
that Ferguson kept dropping him. United, meanwhile,
claimed that David had a bad back – and there was
speculation that the real cause of the problem was the
amount of money he was demanding. David was sanguine.
He went shopping.

In January, Sir Alex put David in the starting line-up for
the first time in seven weeks, in a match against Fulham,
but he was not at his best and was dropped again in the
next match with Newcastle. And the problem with the
contract had still not been resolved. United were aware
that, if they didn't tie David down by January 2003, he
would be free to sign a pre-contract agreement with

another club, but the various advisers simply could not agree. There was not only the money to think about, there were also lucrative image rights. 'Both sides are frustrated,' said United chief executive Peter Kenyon. 'You do reach a point where you can't go further and after several months of good negotiations you also reach a point where you conclude things one way or the other.' The 'other', of course, referred to selling David.

There was at least one step forward in February 2002 when, after months of speculation, Sir Alex Ferguson confirmed that he would be staying on as manager. 'I am over the moon. We had been hearing the rumours about the manager not retiring, but we didn't believe them,' said David. 'But he came in before training on Tuesday and told us.' It emerged that Sir Alex's wife Cathy had persuaded her husband to stay on. 'We all know about wives always making the decisions!' chirped David. He also revealed that negotiations were finally moving forward with his own contract. A salary of £70,000 a week had been agreed and now the two teams had just to sort out image rights.

At the same time, it was turning out to be an action-filled year. It was announced that Victoria was expecting a second baby. Both families were delighted. David's father Ted was in Manchester to watch United play Aston Villa and drove Victoria to the game. 'I wouldn't have thought this will be the end of it,' he said as the family prepared for a champagne celebration. 'Victoria has said she would like a lot of children and I know David would, so I'm sure there will be more.'

The announcement of the pregnancy also meant that David was keener than ever to stay put. 'United is the only environment I've known,' he said. 'I have so many friends around me it's difficult to imagine how I might react to anything else. I'm talking about real friends here, not just workmates.'

Sir Alex was equally eager to finalise contract details and David continued to pay tribute to him. 'Of course, I respect him because, for a start, he's the reason I'm here,' he said. 'And that goes for a lot of the other players here as well. I think we all realise that, without Alex Ferguson, we might not have progressed in the way we have. He's the one who gave us a chance and had faith in us. He believed he had some youngsters who could come all the way through. I think our respect for him stems from that. In spite of what anyone says, there's never been a problem on that score.'

Finally contract negotiations were complete: David was to receive £70,000 a week, with a further £20,000 a week for his image rights. It was a relief for everyone. David was now tied to the club for the foreseeable future – on top of which he was now one of England's best-paid footballers.

As the World Cup approached, all eyes centred on David's every move on the pitch. There were serious fears that he might have been badly injured when he was tackled by Diego Tristan during a match against Deportivo La Coruna and had to be stretchered off. This came right after Sven-Goran Eriksson warned, 'Injuries are the only big worry that I have. If I go to games and see a player on the ground I just cross my fingers.' David's injuries, however, proved less serious than originally thought, with Ferguson commenting, 'He could be back next week.'

It was a relief all round. David had matured so much, both as a person and a player, that playing without him would have been a serious blow. 'I think it would have been a big problem if he was not fit to lead England in this summer's finals,' said England legend Sir Tom Finney. 'He is one of the biggest influences on the rest of the side. He doesn't get involved in silly things like he used to.'

World Cup star Ray Wilkins agreed. 'We would really have suffered without him,' he said. 'He has proved over the last few games that he is a real lucky talisman for England.'

As David recovered from his injury, he could at least console himself with the fact that he was now the richest sports star under the age of 30, overtaking the previous year's incumbent, the boxer Naseem Hamad. Together, he and Victoria were now estimated to be worth £35 million, according to the *Sunday Times* Rich List, where they came in at 962 out of the top 1,000. And he needed the good news. A week later, back playing against Coruna, he was again stretchered off – and this time it was serious. A broken metatarsal bone in his foot meant he would be out of action for six to eight weeks, making him doubtful for the World Cup.

It was ironic. At the end of the previous year, when David had wanted to play, he had been confined to the bench. Now, when Ferguson wanted to play him, he was stuck in a hospital bed. As usual with David, his injury made the front pages. An oxygen tent was installed in the Cheshire apartment to aid David's recovery and he was given ultrasound therapy. Meanwhile, well-wishers were even leaving get-well cards around David's waxwork at Madame Tussaud's. The Prime Minister sent a good-luck message. The world, as usual, went mad.

United without Becks lost out in the title race to Arsenal.

But David's metatarsal made a rapid recovery and he joined the England team flying to Japan for the World Cup. David had chosen Paul Smith suits for the 23 players and they all looked very smart as they trooped on to a specially chartered plane at Luton. They were also presented with goodie bags, with the contents chosen by David, containing £4,000 worth of designer luggage, state-of-the-art laptops and CD players from Sony, and silver Paul Smith cufflinks. The first stop was Dubai, where the team were to spend a few days resting with their wives and children in attendance, before going on to the Far East.

Victoria, who had been planning on staying behind, changed her mind at the last minute and decided to accompany her husband. There were still some anxieties about David's state of health, to say nothing of the fact that he had put on half a stone. He sought to allay the nation's fears. 'It is just a question of regaining my fitness now, and that's not a problem,' he said. 'I put on a little bit of weight, but it won't be a problem getting it off. There are ways of getting my fitness back other than playing in the pre-tournament games against South Korea and Cameroon.

'Kicking a ball won't be a problem but the first time I will take any risk with the foot is in the first game against Sweden. That's the first time I'll risk it in a tackle.'

Japan couldn't wait to welcome David. He is, if anything, an even bigger star in the Land of the Rising Sun than he is in Britain and David knew that, after the stopover in Korea, he was guaranteed the kind of welcome usually reserved for rock stars and royalty.

'I do get a lot of attention but I have never experienced anything like it is when I have been in Japan,' said David.

'It is absolutely mad. You only take one step outside your hotel room and you are surrounded by 50 people in the corridor. I tried to go shopping but they had to literally close the entire shopping centre. There were all kinds of people – kids, girls. It is nice, but mad.'

The madness was about to start again. World Cup 2002 had arrived at last.

10

Tokyo – indeed, the whole of Japan – was going Beckham-mad. Posters of him were dotted all over buses, women's magazines featured him more heavily than ever and his number-seven strip was being bought up by thousands of young fans. They called him Be-Ka-Mu, the nearest version of his name in katakana, the system of characters used by the Japanese to describe foreign words.

Back in Britain, it was the Queen's Golden Jubilee weekend. England was to play Sweden on that Sunday night and Beckham sent out a message to the fans at home. 'I feel proud to be England captain and know that there are so many people back home willing us to do well,' he said. 'Everyone is patriotic about the national team and it has been proved since we qualified. It's a massive weekend. Everyone is going to have a good time and – fingers crossed – everyone will be just that little bit happier on Sunday night.'

He went on to rally his team-mates. 'I've got a feeling my time has come – this will be my proudest moment in football,' he said. 'I am a patriot and to be leading out not just any England team but this England team is going to be a special moment for me. There are no nerves. We are young, talented and hungry. We've got an unbelievable spirit in the camp and only winning interests us. We want the World Cup!'

The match against Sweden turned out to be something of a damp squib, resulting in a 1–1 draw, but David was firmly upbeat as they prepared for their next game –against the old nemesis Argentina. 'We're playing one of the best teams in the world, so we've got to believe in ourselves,' he said.

David led England out against Argentina – and this time it was personal. Four years ago, Argentina had turned David into a hate figure: now was the time for revenge – and he got it. In the 44th minute of the game, England were awarded a penalty kick, and David stepped up to take it. Ignoring the words of 'advice' from Argentina players, and Diego Simeone trying to shake his hand, he tucked his spot kick away to earn England a highly satisfying 1–0 win.

As he scored, the Sapporo stadium erupted. So did the pubs and bars of Britain: city streets had been visibly empty while the match was on as everyone and his wife gathered to watch the match. David's redemption was complete: he was emphatically celebrated as the greatest living Englishman.

'It feels better than it did four years ago and it's just unbelievable,' a jubilant Beckham said after the match. 'It's been four years since the last time and a long four years. So that tops it all off.'

Taking the penalty been an extremely brave act. As David himself admitted, had he missed, against Argentina of all teams, he might well have been back at square one again. But he took the risk – and it paid off.

From that moment, it got better. England went on to draw with Nigeria and then beat Denmark while, to the additional delight of England fans, Argentina crashed out of the World Cup. England were now through to the quarter-finals and there seemed a real chance that they would pull through to the very end.

The outcome of the match against Denmark lifted 'Beckham-mania' to even greater heights. More than 5,000 fans besieged the team bus to get a glimpse of David on the way to training, while the hysteria generated by his appearance meant he wasn't allowed out alone. And, unlike the other players, he didn't even have the consolation of his wife flying out to be with him. All the other wives and girlfriends were coming to Japan – Sven had promised the team this treat if they beat Denmark – except David's.

It turned out that England would be playing Brazil in the quarter-final that Friday – and it was in that match that the dream was shattered. Brazil won 2–1, leaving the entire team devastated, but especially David. He felt he'd let the country down. 'Throughout this competition, I've always had a sneaky feeling that we could go all the way,' he said sadly. 'I told everyone I had this belief we could do it. I thought we had the beating of Brazil, especially in the first half [when England took the lead]. If we had gone in 1–0 up at half-time, who knows what would have happened? Once they got that goal, it was all a different story. It was a terribly difficult time to concede a goal. Then to leak another one straight after half-time made it even harder. In the end, it just wasn't meant to be.'

On his return to England, David cheered up a little bit.

For a start, he was reunited with Victoria and Brooklyn – they had been apart a total of six weeks. And he began to realise that, far from vilifying him, the whole country was proud of its returning son. Meanwhile, his own son greeted him with the words 'I love you so much, Daddy', which did an enormous amount to lift his spirits. Indeed, he felt so much better, he was even able to get Brooklyn's name embroidered in gold on one of the back seats of his new £165,000 Bentley, his 27th birthday present from Victoria.

Clearly planning to stay at United for many years to come, David then bought a £1.25-million barn conversion in Cheshire. With Brooklyn three years old and a new arrival expected shortly, the old flat had just become too small. The new place was just two miles away in Nether Alderley and a spectacular house: it boasted five bedrooms, a gym and a 35-foot pool, as well as half an acre of grounds. It was the perfect place to bring up a family.

Revelling in his new status as national icon, David then participated in the launch of the Commonwealth Games: he met the Queen at the City of Manchester Stadium and in a glittering ceremony handed her the Jubilee Baton.

As if all this were not enough, a huge painting of Beckham was then unveiled in the Pantheon, a classical building at the Stourhead, Wiltshire, a National Trust-owned landscaped garden, as part of a month of displays and events to re-create how the gardens looked 200 years ago. The painting, by Barry Novis, showed David in full England kit, arms raised in triumph, and stood among figures including Hercules, Bacchus, Isis and Diana.

Then, on 1 September 2002, Victoria gave birth to the couple's second son, a 7lb 4oz baby whom they called

Romeo. David was present – having driven down south after playing in Manchester United's 1–1 draw with Sunderland on Wearside the previous day – and emerged from the hospital beaming. 'Romeo's gorgeous. Victoria's great. She's sitting up in bed and the family are here.' And why the unusual name? Because they liked it, David replied.

David lost no time in having his red boots embossed with the name. 'Romeo' was stitched on the tongue just above Brooklyn, in time for the Premiership match against Middlesbrough. Three days later, David escorted Victoria from the hospital, using the usual procedure, involving a couple of cars and the back entrance.

Towards the end of September, David achieved yet another ambition: to captain United in the Champions League against Bayer Leverkusen. It was only to be a one-off as Roy Keane was temporarily away and David had often said he knew he'd never get the position while Keane was there, but it was a testament to the faith that Sir Alex had in him and it made subsequent events all the sadder. It also marked David's tenth year with the club.

'I have to admit, I never had David down as a captain,' said Fergie. 'But the thing that impressed me was how well he responded to being made captain of England, because I honestly never saw him as a leader of that nature. He was always a quiet lad in the dressing room with us. But the way he fitted into the role of leading England has been fantastic and he's improved as a player through that.'

But there was an ominous hint of what was to come. 'I think David's best when he's concentrating on his football with us,' Ferguson continued. 'He has a high profile and it's difficult to say how young people handle that. All I can say on the matter is that David's incredible in the way he handles it all.' Sir Alex may have been paying tribute to David's ability to cope with his high profile, but it looked like he didn't like it.

David remained blithely unaware of the matter and promptly made an appearance in the middle of Manchester wearing something that looked like an Alice band in his hair, but which was actually called a Flexicomb. Onlookers actually stopped and stared. 'It's not the sort of hairdo you'd expect to see on a top footballer,' said one. 'I bet he'll get a lot of stick about it in the Manchester United dressing room.'

It wasn't just the Mancunian shoppers who commented on the new style – yet again, it made almost all the papers. As ever, David shrugged it off.

He and Victoria now could not so much as change their hairstyle without commanding blanket coverage and, given that both were prone to doing just that at the drop of a hat, they were to become more exposed than ever. If anything, the couple seemed to have stepped into the gap left by Princess Diana. They were young, beautiful, vibrant, rich – and, to cap it all, they were in love. As Christmas approached, the Beckhams had Romeo baptised and prepared to face a gruelling year ahead. But David was now so famous he was threatening to become bigger than Manchester United. And, in Sir Alex Ferguson's eyes, no one gets bigger than the club.

11

At the start of 2003, it seemed nothing could mar David's golden existence. Victoria and the children were at the centre of his life, he was at the peak of his powers as a footballer and he was, to put it bluntly, rolling in it. At £3.5 million a year from United, he was one of the best-paid footballers in the country and his sponsorship deals now included Police sunglasses, Brylcreem, Marks & Spencer, Vodafone, Adidas, Pepsi and Rage Software. He had three houses, each one a mansion, a vast car collection and everything in the world to look forward to. What could possibly go wrong?

David starred in an advertisement for Pepsi that also featured Real Madrid's goalkeeper, Iker Casillas. The two could have had no idea that just six months later they would be team-mates.

A study called 'One David Beckham: Celebrity, Masculinity and the Soccerati' by Dr Andrew Parker of Warwick University and Professor Ellis Cashmore of Staffordshire University concluded that David was the most influential man in Britain. That wouldn't have gone down well with his club manager. Whatever the state of the tough old Glaswegian's feelings, it was less than a week after all this that a football boot flew through the air and connected with David's forehead. From that moment on, there was no going back. When it was finally time to go, the decision was not Victoria's, nor even David's. It was down to Sir Alex.

The end of David's career at Manchester United, when it came, was brutal. In the summer of 2003, the Beckhams were in Los Angeles to present an MTV award, part of their 'World Tour'. On 10 June, David's agent, Tony Stephens, told him to look at the Man United website. What he saw was breathtaking in its abruptness:

Manchester United have released the following statement regarding David Beckham and Barcelona: 'Manchester United confirms that club officials have met Joan Laporta, the leading candidate for the presidency of Barcelona. These meetings have resulted in an offer being made for the transfer for David Beckham to Barcelona. This offer is subject to a number of conditions and critically to Mr Laporta being elected president on Sunday 15 June and Barcelona subsequently reaching agreement with David Beckham on his personal contract. Manchester United confirms that in the event that all of the conditions are fulfilled, then the offer would be acceptable.

SFX issued its own statement on behalf of its client: 'David is very disappointed and surprised to learn of this statement and feels that he has been used as a political pawn in the

Barcelona presidential elections. David's advisors have no plans to meet Mr Laporta or his representatives.'

Nor was David's father, Ted, particularly pleased. 'I shall tell him not to go there,' he said. 'I don't want him to go just because a certain person wants him to go.' But alas, when that certain person was Sir Alex Ferguson, Becks had no choice.

The writing had been on the wall for months, if not years. Fergie had frequently and publicly criticised David's celebrity lifestyle, but it was in February 2003 that matters really got out of hand. United lost 2–0 at home to Arsenal, after which Fergie, angry at the team's performance, stormed into the dressing room and kicked a boot. To everyone's horror, it flew at David and struck him in the face, cutting him above the eye. Sir Alex initially described it as a 'freakish accident', but there was no way back from there.

The Barcelona statement had almost certainly been made to open a bidding war, and so it proved. Real Madrid came in with a rival bid and the two Spanish giants went head to head. United's chief executive Peter Kenyon and managing director Peter Gill met representatives from Real Madrid in Sardinia and, shortly afterwards, on 17 June, an announcement was made. Becks was moving to Madrid in a deal worth £25 million to United and £30 million to Beckham himself. The contract was set for four years, during which time he would be earning £120,000 a week.

David greeted the end of his relationship with Alex Ferguson with good grace. 'I would like to publicly thank Sir Alex Ferguson for making me the player I am today,' he said. 'I will always hold precious memories of my time at

Manchester United and Old Trafford, as well as the players, who I regard as part of my family, and the brilliant fans who have given me so much support over the years.'

In victory, Sir Alex could also afford to be magnanimous, issuing a statement of congratulations and best wishes for the future. There were mutters from quite a few commentators – and Ted Beckham – that David had been treated shabbily, but the die was now cast.

And so the Beckhams began to plan their move. They enjoyed a brief holiday in the South of France, before David embarked on a tour of Asia with his new club. Victoria, in what was to set the tone of the early days in Madrid, stayed behind in England for a meeting with the Spice Girls' Svengali Simon Fuller, in an attempt to restart her career, this time round by promoting 'Brand Beckham'.

The family moved to Madrid at the end of the summer, initially staying in hotels while they began to search for a house. David gave happy interviews, explaining that he would miss family and friends as well as 'pie and mash and jellied eels', but saying that he was looking forward to his new life. However, in retrospect, it is clear that for possibly the first time in their marriage, he and Victoria had either failed to think through the full implications of the move, or had thought, erroneously, that each had reached an accommodation with the other. Whatever the case, David was asked if Victoria would be accompanying him to Madrid. 'That's what we have to do,' he said. 'We have to fully commit ourselves to Spain and to Real Madrid, and that's what we're doing.' Or was it?

David's first appearance with his new team was judged to be a great success, while his new team-mates were exposed for the first time to the full force of the media whirlwind that was Brand Beckham. The club's Hongta Sports press room was too small to hold the assortment of international journalists covering the team's first public statement with Beckham in their midst: David professed himself to be happy and beginning to learn a few words of Spanish.

But David was living in a foreign country with a language he didn't understand, new team-mates, who were acquaintances rather than friends, with no home of his own to stay in and only the comforts of a hotel. Nor did it ring any warning bells with anyone when an attractive young woman called Rebecca Loos was assigned to look after him.

In October, there was an upset when David was pictured at a Madrid nightclub, without Victoria, but with a group of other people, including Rebecca Loos. Shortly afterwards, Rebecca was quietly moved to another role. David then parted company with SFX management, amid frenzied speculation that he was to cut down on his promotional work, which was by now earning him about £24 million a year. He wanted to focus on football.

But in April came the news that was to test their marriage to the full. Rebecca Loos alleged that she had had a brief fling with David, a story that changed his image completely overnight.

Though the Beckham marriage had been tested it appeared to be withstanding the impact. Asked about England's preparations for Euro 2004 by a Sky reporter, Beckham took the opportunity to deal with the mud that had been slung at him over the affair. 'I've been called a bad father, I've been called a bad husband and my wife has been called a bad mother. Things always hurt that are said about my family, and for people to call my wife a bad mother is unbelievable. I'm a strong person, I'm a strong family man, I'm a strong husband and a strong father.'

But the rumours didn't just stop and Euro 2004 offered no escape. David missed two crucial penalties, one as England lost to France in the opening game and another in the quarter-final shoot-out defeat against Portugal. Was his personal life affecting his professional career after all?

Talking to BBC's *Match of the Day*, David acknowledged that he had been under a great deal of stress. 'A lot of things were said about me last season that were not true,' he said. 'Looking back on it, I can see that maybe I was taking what was happening on and off the pitch with me onto the pitch in Portugal and that my performances may have suffered slightly. We are together as a family in Madrid now and that is wonderful. They were actually out here more last season than some people thought but we had trouble finding the right school for Brooklyn. Now we have got a school for him and a playgroup for Romeo, while Victoria is working from Madrid.'

It was not – by a long shot – to be the end of the rumours and speculation, but it was a start. More than anything else, despite having an even more torrid time of it than the two were used to, David and Victoria had at least shown the world their determination to stay together and keep their relationship strong. In late August it was announced that Victoria was expecting their third child – and they were planning to have the baby in Spain.

To begin with, at least, 2005 looked as if it was going to

be rather calmer than the year that had preceded it. On 20 February, Victoria gave birth to the couple's third son, Cruz, at the Ruber International Hospital in Madrid. David radiated happiness as he divulged the news. There was some comment when David missed Victoria's birthday in April, although in truth there was nothing more sinister behind it than that he was playing in a match 200 miles away. The calm, however, did not last long.

Their former nanny, Abbie Gibson, decided to tell a Sunday newspaper about domestic life with the Beckhams. Victoria, straight to the point as always, called Abbie a 'two-faced cow'. 'Yeah, we have our arguments, of course we do – but all couples row, don't they? So at least it makes us bloody normal. To be honest, I'm more sad that this happened now, because me and David are really happy.'

David was equally livid. 'I'm being portrayed as some kind of uncaring monster and Victoria is meant to be the Wicked Witch of the West,' he snapped. 'I am sick of it. It's just people selling stories for money. I'm sick and tired of everybody having a go at us just for being a normal couple. We're happily married and are going to stay that way.'

12

Behind all the nonsense, it was business as usual. Having announced that she was giving up singing, Victoria was now pursuing a career in fashion, while David followed his dream of opening up a fleet of sports academies across the world. One academy was already open in London and now he was to be the partner in a similar one in Los Angeles. He joined Simon Fuller and Tim Leiweke, the president and chief executive of Anschutz Entertainment Group, to reveal the plans. 'It's about kids coming down, getting off the streets, having fun,' he said.

Asked if he might one day consider a full-time move to the United States, David was enthusiastic. 'Yeah, I think it's always a possibility,' he admitted. 'In my career, things have happened and situations have happened and I never, ever thought that I'd be playing anywhere apart from England. But I'm playing in Spain now, and there is an opportunity to come to America, and I am thinking about it, definitely.' It would probably be easier for Victoria to adapt to the States than it had been for her to get used to Spain, too.

While the couple were in LA, they were invited to the home of their new friend, Tom Cruise. And Becks' appeal appeared to be withstanding the nannygate revelations. In May he was wheeled out as one of the most high profile supporters for London to gain the Olympics in 2012, appearing alongside the then Prime Minister Tony Blair and Lord Coe, the bid chairman, at a presentation in Singapore. 'We back the bid because we believe it will inspire young people and give them the chance to see an Olympics in our own country,' said David, speaking alongside Victoria.

Another World Cup was now looming and the couple had planned a pre-World Cup party: the Full Length and Fabulous Ball, to take place on 21 May 2006. Robbie Williams and James Brown provided the music, while Gordon Ramsay was in charge of catering. The guest list included Tom Cruise, Liz Hurley, Sir Elton John, the Osbournes, Ewan McGregor, Kate Moss and Elle Macpherson.

The World Cup turned out to be something of a damp squib, with a lacklustre England failing to shine, never more so than when they played Portugal in the quarter-final and lost. Beckham had been forced to leave the pitch in the 52nd minute due to an Achilles injury. England went on to lose on penalties. The country's faith in Sven Goran Eriksson had run out, and there were question marks over David's fitness to captain the side.

With characteristic good grace, he took the decision to step down. 'I feel the time is right to pass on the armband as we enter a new era under new coach Steve McClaren,' he said. But McClaren didn't reciprocate; deciding instead to stamp his mark on the job by dropping David from the squad altogether, something Becks had not expected.

'He [McClaren] called me when I was getting on a plane for 15 hours to America ... and he said there's going to be casualties along the way and unfortunately you're one of the casualties,' David later revealed. 'It surprised me, I must admit, and I am gutted 'cos playing for England was everything to me. I still hope that I'm going to play for England again – I don't want to retire from international football.' He added, 'If I was a betting man I wouldn't bet on me playing again, but who knows?'

Many people were betting on him never playing again. They underestimated David's determination and what England meant to him.

With David's footballing career entering its autumn years, clearly the duo were now beginning to think more carefully about what the future held. Both liked the United States and it was becoming obvious that that was where the opportunities for each of them lay. There were rumours that David had been in talks with Philip Anschutz about joining the New York Red Bulls, while Victoria was said to be keen to launch a fashion series on US TV.

It was with that pragmatic thought in mind that Becks accepted a £128 million five-year deal to play for the American team LA Galaxy at the beginning of 2007. The move made various records, with David set to earn a staggering £500,000 a week, although he was adamant it was not the financial rewards that were to take him Stateside. 'It's the right time for us to do it,' he explained. 'I don't want to go out to America when I'm 34 years old with people turning round and saying, "Well, he's only going there to get the money."'

Timothy Leiweke, president of Anschutz Entertainment

Group, which owns LA Galaxy, was delighted with the move. 'David Beckham will have a greater impact on soccer in America than any athlete has ever had on a brand globally,' he claimed.

First, though, he had six months of his contract with Real Madrid to run, and the club was insisting he see it out – even though coach Fabio Capello declared that he would not play for the team again. But he was forced – largely by fan power – to go back on that promise, and when he brought David back in, the football world saw a rejuvenated Beckham, properly rested and firing on all cylinders. Now people started to bemoan the fact that far from his best years being behind him, David Beckham was as good as he'd ever had been – and was going to waste all that talent on an American club. He couldn't win, but seemed remarkably unperturbed by the furore raging about him once more.

England manager Steve McClaren, who had been Alex Ferguson's assistant at Manchester United when they won the treble in 1999, was also having a rethink. 'We have four weeks before the squad is announced [for the Euro 2008 qualifiers] and we will see what happens,' he said. 'He is performing well for his club – obviously that's a problem I would rather have than not have. He has always bounced back from every adversity in his career. It's pleasing to see that a month ago he would never play for Real Madrid again and there he is starring in a game against Bayern Munich and being man of the match.'

David himself was well aware of the debate. 'Football is all about opinions and I know there are some who don't want me in the squad,' he admitted. 'But if people think my

England career is over, I want to show it isn't. I'm the underdog now. Eight months ago it was being said that I shouldn't be in the England team any more and my career was over. Even if I look back two or three weeks I wasn't playing for Real Madrid and all of a sudden it's turned around. Of course, things would be different if England were winning and almost qualified for Euro 2008, but people always look for other options. I'm not going to lie – I love the fact that I have got the backing of the public – it's a great feeling. We love it in England when we see players determined to prove people wrong. We love it when people fight back – and I've always tried to do that.'

David and Sir Alex also buried the hatchet when the former United man was invited to Old Trafford to play in a charity game to celebrate United's 50 years in Europe, and although injury stopped him from playing, he was treated as an honoured guest. 'It's amazing to be back – I've waited four years for this,' he told the fans. 'I'm devastated I couldn't play, but I wanted to see everyone again and say, "Thank you". Everyone knows you've got the best manager in the world at this club. I've watched the majority of United's games this season on TV in Spain and I'm sure they are going to go on and win many trophies.'

'It's nice of David to say that,' said an equally gracious Ferguson. 'I expected him to get a great reception from the fans – he was a great player for us.'

Shortly afterwards, McClaren named him in the England team to play Brazil in a friendly to mark the opening of the new Wembley Stadium. David played well and set up England's goal in a 1–1 draw. He was picked again to play Estonia in a Euro 2008 qualifier, and set up two of England's goals in a 3–0 win. But his presence was not enough to prevent a 3–2 home defeat to Croatia, which meant England failed to qualify and McClaren's reign was over.

By now his form had prompted comments of regret and jubilation in Madrid and LA respectively. 'We have all made mistakes regarding Beckham,' said Real president Ramon Calderon. 'Beckham is a great player now he is playing at the same level he did at Manchester. He has recovered his physical and psychological condition because he was upset not to be playing with his national team.'

LA Galaxy 'politely but firmly' rejected attempts by Real to buy him out of his contract. 'Nothing has changed,' said Alexi Lalas, general manager of LA Galaxy. 'We can't wait for Beckham to get here. Real's hopes about keeping Beckham are benign – that ship has sailed.'

David's last game in Madrid was a triumph: he helped Real to beat Real Mallorca 3–1, as his friend Tom Cruise watched in the crowd. For Capello, it wasn't such an auspicious end to the season. He was sacked as Real Madrid coach – but his association with David was by no means over.

Meanwhile, Victoria had news of her own – shortly before the family finally made their move to LA, it was announced that the Spice Girls would be reuniting at the end of the year. David, of course, would be there offering his support. The Beckhams' profile, already stratospheric, was about to get bigger still.

13

The arrival of the Beckhams in America resembled a state visit from a reigning monarch. The couple had transcended what might be called the rational celebrity they deserved – they had become a brand. Not even the sum of their two parts any longer, the couple had achieved über-fame, and their new countrymen were ecstatic to have them there at long last.

They prefaced the move by an interview in W Magazine, which made world headlines because of its raunchy shots of the pair: one photo had Victoria reclining on the bonnet of a car as David stood over her. It captured headlines across the world. They were quizzed on their new £11 million mansion in Beverly Hills – Victoria did the house-hunting, sending pictures of each room to David on her mobile phone. It was a 13,000 square foot, six-bedroom villa with pool, tennis court and screening room but not, she insisted, too over-the-top.

The world's press converged on LA Galaxy as David held a press conference to announce his arrival. 'Thank you for making my dream come true,' he began. 'My family have now moved to Los Angeles and it is something we look forward to and are proud of. In our life, everything is perfect. The most important thing in my life is my family, but the second is football – sorry soccer. I have to get used to that. In my career I have played for two of the biggest clubs in the world in Manchester United and Real Madrid. I have played for my country for the last 11 years, and I still am. I have always looked for challenges and something exciting, and this is one of the biggest challenges I have ever taken in my career. Soccer in America could potentially be as big as anywhere in the world. I am proud to be part of trying to help the sport grow for the next five years and possibly longer.' Possibly longer... It was a clear sign that the family were sure where their future lay.

'The hype is there at the moment and the hype will be there for maybe six months,' he said in an interview with *Sports Illustrated*. 'But to keep the interest in soccer, that's going to be the challenge. I'm not silly enough to think I'm going to change the whole culture, because it's not going to happen. But I do have a belief that soccer can go to a different level and I'd love to be a part of that. People do think they're going to see me turn out and we'll win our first game 10–0. That's one thing I'm worried about. I'm not a player who will run past ten players and score three or four goals. My game is about working hard, being a team player and assists.'

Indeed, Beckham was being spoken of as not just the saviour of LA Galaxy, but the man who would transform the status of American soccer – it was an awfully big burden for one person to bear. His new team put in a dreadful performance shortly after his arrival, losing 3–0 to the not-very-good Mexican team Tigres. He was unable to play due to a strained ankle, but watched the game with a slightly shocked air.

But Hollywood was overjoyed to welcome the new arrivals. Their new friends Tom Cruise and Katie Holmes hosted a party in their honour at the Museum of Contemporary Art's Geffen Contemporary Gallery, which was so A-list it made the Oscars appear devoid of stars. Attendees included Will Smith, Demi Moore, Bruce Willis, Jim Carrey, Eva Longoria and Brooke Shields. The doubters could say what they liked about David's new team, but when it came to what Hollywood really recognised – celebrity and wealth – the Beckhams had arrived at their spiritual home.

The Brazilian footballer Pele, widely regarded as the greatest player ever, offered the benefit of his experience trying to do the same thing as David with New York Cosmos, 30-odd years previously. 'I would advise him to be very well prepared for the matches. I know the level of play in the league. It is well balanced and the spectators will demand a lot from him as their star player. But when there's no training or practice, then he can stroll through Hollywood.'

Sir Alex Ferguson was also sceptical. 'They have already had Pele, Cruyff and Beckenbauer out there,' he said. 'I don't know what kind of impact David can make. He can't change the whole country, and the sheer size of the place makes it more difficult.'

And indeed, the soccer was not going so well. There was mounting dissatisfaction from the fans that David's sprained ankle had kept him off the field and so, although it was not yet healed, he finally made an appearance in the

78th minute of a game, touching the ball only 12 times. The man said to be behind his appearance was Simon Fuller, he who had first introduced the Spice Girls to the world, and it was Fuller who now managed Brand Beckham.

'Brand Beckham needed their star on the field and Simon made sure it happened,' said a source. 'For the thousands of extra seats sold that day, the hundreds of thousands of seats sold at stadiums across America anticipating Beckham's arrival, for all the licensed merchandise, endorsements and to keep the hype alive, he needed to be on the field. And Simon is producing a new TV series following Beckham's progress in American soccer, which began airing this week. It would be a disappointing premiere if Beckham spent his first game on the sidelines icing his ankle – that's not exciting TV.'

But as David worked hard to regain full fitness, the surreal nature of his and Victoria's adventure was put into sharp perspective when his father Ted, then 59, suffered a heart attack. The entire clan rushed to Ted's bedside – at Whipps Cross Hospital in east London. Ted made a rapid recovery and four days after they arrived in London, the Beckhams were able to return to LA.

But it had been a salutary warning about what was really important in the couple's lives. David and Ted had already been partially reconciled after rows following his divorce from Sandra and the publication by Ted of a book, but father and son were now close once more. Ted acknowledged as much. 'All three of my children – David, Lynne and Joanne – have been a tower of strength,' he said. 'They have helped me get through this, along with the doctors and nurses. I owe a lot to all of them.'

As the year drew to a close, David was one of a very select few to appear on Michael Parkinson's last-ever chat show, along with Billy Connolly and Dame Judi Dench, confirming his growing status as national treasure. He had also, courtesy of the Croatia match, won his 99th cap for England and now seemed almost assured of his much-coveted 100th when he was named as the official face of the FA's bid to host the World Cup in 2018. Given that he had also been involved in England's successful bid to host the 2012 Olympics, clearly he was now a well-regarded figure within the sporting establishment, as well as one of its greatest players.

On *Parkinson*, he talked emotionally about stepping down as England captain. 'I remember waking up that morning and I cried as I knew what I was going to have to do,' he said. 'I went into the Press conference, cried all the way down to it, got through it and cried all the way back to the hotel. But I have had a great career on the England side. [But] I won't be retiring yet. I believe I have two or three years yet, but I will never be a manager.'

While his contemporaries were retiring from international football, Becks refused to give up on his country. It had been his boyhood dream and he had never lost that enthusiasm.

He wasn't above putting on a rather bold front, however. In December 2007, he signed a three-year, £20 million contract to become a designer's 'ambassador' for Armani, and his first appearance for the brand was an eye-popping one. David appeared with what was termed the 'Goldenballs lunchbox' right out there, in a bulging pair of skimpy briefs. The picture didn't leave a lot to the imagination. Sales of Armani underwear rose by a staggering 30 per cent, while sales of men's underwear generally soared. It was the Beckham effect in action once again.

Among the football writers the big question was whether David would ever be awarded the landmark 100th cap for England – or indeed whether he deserved to. While his brilliance in dead ball situations was universally acknowledged, there were those who felt a younger generation of faster, trickier wide midfielders should be brought in in his place. But one man who still rated his overall abilities very highly was his former manager at Real Madrid, Fabio Capello. And guess who had just been named the new England manager?

Meanwhile, LA Galaxy was already feeling the benefit of the Beckham effect. 300,000 Beckham jerseys had been sold, with sales of shirts 700 times more than usual. 'Merchandise sales overall have gone up two or three times,' said Don Gerber, head of Major League Soccer. 'International TV sales have gone up from next to nothing to distribution in 100 countries, with live games in Asia and Mexico. Major League Soccer has more global awareness than at any other time in our history because of David. But the real value we've yet to realise is the impact David will have on the field. He's been injured, but we look forward to him having another first year in MLS in 2008.'

14

Christmas 2007 was spent back in the UK. The newly reformed Spice Girls were performing in London and Beckingham Palace was convenient for all the parents, so it was natural the family should be in residence for the time of year. They all seemed to be enjoying it: a proud David was spotted skating with Romeo at the Winter Wonderland rink in London's Hyde Park – Victoria stayed at the side.

Fabio Capello kept the pundits guessing over David's 100th cap when he left him out of the England squad for his first game in charge, a friendly against Switzerland on 6 February. But on 26 March he ended the speculation by starting him in a friendly against France in Paris. David played for an hour in the 1–0 defeat, a performance that didn't go far enough to convince the sceptics that this was anything more than a token gesture from Capello to grant Becks the honour of joining Billy Wright, Bobby Charlton, Bobby Moore and Peter Shilton on reaching this remarkable landmark.

With the MLS season having ended in October, Becks had been training with Arsenal to get himself fit enough for

England, fuelling speculation that a move to the north London club might be on the cards. But he returned to LA Galaxy in the spring, for his first full MLS season. Fit and on form, he began to show the American fans what all the fuss had been about. On 26 May, in a 3–1 win against Kansas City Wizards, he scored from 70 yards, rekindling memories of the goal he had scored from the half-way line against Wimbledon all those years ago in 1996.

But doing well for LA Galaxy wasn't enough for Becks. His commitment to England was as strong as ever, and Fabio Capello had given him every incentive to push for a regular place in the team. There was a World Cup to qualify for, and Capello knew that David could be a key ingredient – his skills and experience making him a unique figure in the England squad.

'I don't look at age, I look at qualities and Beckham has lots,' Capello told *La Gazzetta dello Sport*. 'He's serious, he's a great professional and the World Cup is incredibly important to him.'

Two years previously, it had appeared that the 2006 World Cup spelled the end of his international career. Now he was confounding all his critics by playing his way into contention for the 2010 World Cup in South Africa – provided England could qualify.

While half of Europe was concentrating on Euro 2008, Capello set about testing his resources for the challenge ahead, with friendlies against the USA and Trinidad and Tobago. David, in excellent shape both physically and psychologically, played in both, and indeed captained the side in the latter – albeit a temporary appointment.

On 15 October, Becks returned to competitive action for

England in their fourth World Cup qualifier, a 3–1 victory over Belarus in Minsk. Capello had confirmed that Beckham's recall had not been a token gesture, but with the MLS season coming to an end, how would Becks stay in contention as the qualifying campaign moved into 2009?

The answer came as something of a surprise – and must have brought a smile to Victoria's face, after all the previous speculation about her trying to coax her husband from Manchester to somewhere warmer and more fashionable. AC Milan announced that David would be going there on loan during the MLS closed season. On 11 January 2009, he made his debut in a 2–2 draw, his 89 minutes on the pitch proving that Milan boss Carlo Ancelotti was taking him as seriously as England manager Capello.

As the World Cup qualifying campaign got off to a perfect start with four straight wins, David's haul of England caps continued to grow. In a friendly against Slovakia on 28 March, he earned his 109th cap, becoming England's most-capped outfield player, with only Peter Shilton on 125 to surpass for the outright record.

Sir Bobby Charlton was one of those who praised David's long service to the national team. 'David Beckham can't do any more than go on the field and do his best,' he said. 'And his best has been good enough.'

AC Milan agreed a deal with LA Galaxy to extend his loan period until July, something that angered a number of fans in America. On his return to action in the States, David was accused of being a 'fraud' and a 'part-timer' by some fans, but as he had done so many times in his career, he handled the criticism by rolling his sleeves up and working hard. LA Galaxy won the Western Conference final and then went agonisingly close to winning the MLS final, losing to Real Salt Lake 5–4 on penalties after a 1–1 draw. The curse of penalties again – but this time at least Becks had scored with his spot kick.

All in all it had been a good year on the pitch for Becks. England under Capello had qualified for the 2010 World Cup in fine style, a 1–0 defeat in Ukraine after qualification had been confirmed being the only blot on an otherwise perfect record. David returned to Milan in January 2010 for a second loan spell and continued to earn rave reviews for the 'rossoneri'. After his first game back, new AC Milan coach Leonardo praised him to the skies, saying, 'He has an absolute willingness to help. He had a week where we tried him in every role. He has extraordinary quality and tactical intelligence.'

It was clear that David's rehabilitation at the pinnacle of world football was absolute. Indeed, in his own mind he had never gone away. While others had been quick to write him off, seeing his move to America as a cushy step into retirement for a player who could no longer cut it on the world stage, Becks had shown his determination by working hard, wherever and whenever he could, and the more astute coaches in the business had been bright enough to see that he was anything but a has-been.

The public followed suit. When John Terry lost the England captaincy after newspaper reports of his alleged affair with the ex-girlfriend of England team-mate Wayne Bridge hit the headlines in February, Becks was one of the favourites to assume the captain's armband. In the end, Capello handed it to vice captain Rio Ferdinand, but come the World Cup in South Africa Capello will need more than one leader on the pitch. And David Beckham, with his 'absolute willingness to help' and his 'extraordinary quality and tactical intelligence', will be a key player in England's campaign.